D0579783

DATE DUE

APR 1 3 2011		

Inside SCIENCE

Space Research

Other titles in the *Inside Science* series:

Climate Change Research
Gene Therapy Research
Renewable Energy Research
Stem Cell Research
Vaccine Research

Inside SCIENCE

Space Research

Peggy J. Parks

ReferencePoint Press®

San Diego, CA

© 2011 ReferencePoint Press, Inc.

For more information, contact:
ReferencePoint Press, Inc.
PO Box 27779
San Diego, CA 92198
www.ReferencePointPress.com

LIBRARY OF CONGRESS CATALOGING-IN-PUBLICATION DATA

Parks, Peggy J., 1951–
  Space research / by Peggy J. Parks.
    p. cm. — (Inside science)
  Includes bibliographical references and index.
  ISBN-13: 978-1-60152-111-8 (hardback)
  ISBN-10: 1-60152-111-1 (hardback)
  1. Astronautics—Juvenile literature. 2. Outer space—Exploration—Juvenile literature.
  3. Space sciences—Juvenile literature. I. Title.
  TL793.P326 2011
  500.5—dc22
                                                              2009048159

Contents

Foreword

In 2008, when the Yale Project on Climate Change and the George Mason University Center for Climate Change Communication asked Americans, "Do you think that global warming is happening?" 71 percent of those polled—a significant majority—answered "yes." When the poll was repeated in 2010, only 57 percent of respondents said they believed that global warming was happening. Other recent polls have reported a similar shift in public opinion about climate change.

Although respected scientists and scientific organizations worldwide warn that a buildup of greenhouse gases, mainly caused by human activities, is bringing about potentially dangerous and long-term changes in Earth's climate, it appears that doubt is growing among the general public. What happened to bring about this change in attitude over such a short period of time? Climate change skeptics claim that scientists have greatly overstated the degree and the dangers of global warming. Others argue that powerful special interests are minimizing the problem for political gain. Unlike experiments conducted under strictly controlled conditions in a lab or petri dish, scientific theories, facts, and findings on such a critical topic as climate change are often subject to personal, political, and media bias—whether for good or for ill.

At its core, however, scientific research is not about politics or 30-second sound bites. Scientific research is about questions and measurable observations. Science is the process of discovery and the means for developing a better understanding of ourselves and the world around us. Science strives for facts and conclusions unencumbered by bias, distortion, and political sensibilities. Although sometimes the methods and motivations are flawed, science attempts to develop a body of knowledge that can guide decision makers, enhance daily life, and lay a foundation to aid future generations.

The relevance and the implications of scientific research are profound, as members of the National Academy of Sciences point out in the 2009 edition of *On Being a Scientist: A Guide to Responsible Conduct in Research:*

Some scientific results directly affect the health and well-being of individuals, as in the case of clinical trials or toxicological studies. Science also is used by policy makers and voters to make informed decisions on such pressing issues as climate change, stem cell research, and the mitigation of natural hazards. . . . And even when scientific results have no immediate applications—as when research reveals new information about the universe or the fundamental constituents of matter—new knowledge speaks to our sense of wonder and paves the way for future advances.

The *Inside Science* series provides students with a sense of the painstaking work that goes into scientific research—whether its focus is microscopic cells cultured in a lab or planets far beyond the solar system. Each book in the series examines how scientists work and where that work leads them. Sometimes, the results are positive. Such was the case for Edwin McClure, a once-active high school senior diagnosed with multiple sclerosis, a degenerative disease that leads to difficulties with coordination, speech, and mobility. Thanks to stem cell therapy, in 2009 a healthier McClure strode across a stage to accept his diploma from Virginia Commonwealth University. In some cases, cutting-edge experimental treatments fail with tragic results. This is what occurred in 1999 when 18-year-old Jesse Gelsinger, born with a rare liver disease, died four days after undergoing a newly developed gene therapy technique. Such failures may temporarily halt research, as happened in the Gelsinger case, to allow for investigation and revision. In this and other instances, however, research resumes, often with renewed determination to find answers and solve problems.

Through clear and vivid narrative, carefully selected anecdotes, and direct quotations each book in the *Inside Science* series reinforces the role of scientific research in advancing knowledge and creating a better world. By developing an understanding of science, the responsibilities of the scientist, and how scientific research affects society, today's students will be better prepared for the critical challenges that await them. As members of the National Academy of Sciences state: "The values on which science is based—including honesty, fairness, collegiality, and openness—serve as guides to action in everyday life as well as in research. These values have helped produce a scientific enterprise of unparalleled usefulness, productivity, and creativity. So long as these values are honored, science—and the society it serves—will prosper."

Important Events in Space Research

1962
Astronaut John H. Glenn Jr. becomes the first American to orbit the Earth.

1969
The United States launches *Apollo 11*, and astronauts Neil Armstrong and Buzz Aldrin become the first humans to walk on the moon.

1961
Russian cosmonaut Yuri A. Gagarin, the first human being to travel into space, orbits the Earth once and returns safely.

1926
Scientist Robert Goddard launches the world's first liquid-fueled rocket. He later becomes known as the father of modern rocket propulsion.

1920   **1940**   **1960**   **1980**

1957
The Soviet Union launches *Sputnik*, the world's first artificial satellite.

1963
Valentina Tereshkova, a former textile worker from the Soviet Union, becomes the world's first woman to travel into space.

1958
A civilian space agency is formed in the United States; it later becomes known as the National Aeronautics and Space Administration (NASA).

1981
The United States launches the space shuttle *Columbia*, which is the first reusable spacecraft and the first that is able to land at an ordinary airfield.

1983
Astronaut Sally Ride becomes the first American woman in space when she flies aboard the space shuttle *Challenger*.

2010
President Barack Obama announces his plans for the U.S. space program, including a spacecraft to transport astronauts to and from the International Space Station, extending the life of the space station until at least 2020, and a manned voyage to Mars by the mid-2030s.

1986
The space shuttle *Challenger* disintegrates 73 seconds into flight, killing all seven crew members.

2003
The space shuttle *Columbia* disintegrates when it hits Earth's atmosphere, killing all seven crew members. NASA puts a temporary halt on manned space missions until a review board can investigate the accident.

2006
NASA announces its Constellation Program, a mission that is intended to send astronauts back to the moon.

1996
American astronaut Shannon Lucid sets the world record for time in space by a woman after spending 188 days in space, mostly aboard the Russian space station Mir.

1985   **1990**   **1995**   **2000**   **2005**

1998
The first two modules of the International Space Station are launched and assembled in space by American astronauts and Russian cosmonauts.

1990
The Hubble Space Telescope is launched into orbit by astronauts on the space shuttle *Discovery*.

2004
The Mars Exploration Rovers *Spirit* and *Opportunity* arrive on Mars in separate spacecraft and begin a long-term exploration of the planet.

2009
NASA's Spitzer Space Telescope discovers an enormous ring, which was previously unknown to scientists, around the planet Saturn.

1984
Svetlana Savitskaya, a Soviet cosmonaut, becomes the first woman to walk in space.

"Discovery, Science, Innovation"

On October 9, 2009, officials from the National Aeronautics and Space Administration (NASA) announced that a rocket had crashed into a dark crater on the moon—and it was no accident. For years scientists had been fairly certain that there was some form of water on the moon, but they had not found any proof. So NASA decided to launch a rather unusual mission in order to confirm whether their belief was true. A spacecraft known as the Lunar Crater Observation and Sensing Satellite would be carried to the moon by a rocket called Centaur. Once the spacecraft reached lunar orbit, the rocket would separate and then head straight toward the moon's surface.

After traveling at the incredible speed of 5,600 miles per hour (9,012kph), Centaur slammed into the moon's south polar region. The impact sent up a gigantic cloud of dust and debris known as a plume. A few minutes later the satellite, outfitted with high-powered cameras and other sophisticated instruments, flew into the plume and began taking measurements of the lunar material. It beamed the data back to NASA before it also crashed onto the moon's surface.

Over a period of weeks, scientists analyzed the information and were ecstatic over what they found. Their long-held beliefs proved to be correct—there is indeed water on the moon in the form of ice and water vapor, and it is much more plentiful than anyone could have realized. Peter Schultz, who is a planetary scientist at Brown University, explains the importance of this discovery: "After the Apollo program ended [in 1972], we concluded that the moon was dead. Now what we're seeing is a place with a reservoir of ices that have been collected over billions of years."[1]

The confirmation that there is water on the moon is significant because of what it could mean for future space research. For instance, if the decision is made for astronauts to return to the moon and create a permanent human settlement, finding lunar water sets the stage for this. Joan Vernikos, who is the former director of NASA's Life Sciences

Division, believes that colonies on the moon and elsewhere in space are a distinct possibility. She explains: "It is highly probable that, in this century, humans will settle on other planets. Our ability to explore and sustain human presence there will not only expand Earth's access to mineral resources but, should the need arise, provide alternative habitats for humanity's survival."[2]

Robotic Discoveries

Along with what scientists have learned about the moon, space research has helped increase their understanding of distant planets both in and beyond our solar system. This has been possible because of unmanned spacecraft known as probes, which can travel millions of miles into deep space on journeys that take months or even years. Outfitted with sophisticated cameras and other high-tech equipment, probes have scoured the vast expanse of the universe, making observations, snapping photographs,

Unmanned spacecraft have traveled throughout the solar system (pictured in a computer illustration) and into the vast reaches of space collecting information that has greatly enhanced human understanding of the universe.

and recording measurements. After this information has been gathered, it is beamed back to scientists on Earth.

In December 2009 NASA released data from its *Cassini* probe, which is studying Jupiter and Saturn. The information transmitted by the probe suggests that two of the planets' moons have ice particles, water vapor, and trace organic compounds—conditions that could possibly make them suitable for life. Francis Nimmo, who is a professor of Earth and planetary sciences at the University of California at Santa Cruz, says that this finding does not guarantee that life exists on either of the moons, but it raises the possibility. He explains: "If these moons are habitable, it changes the whole idea of the habitable zone. It changes our thinking about how and where we might find life outside of the solar system."[3]

Humans in Space

As valuable as probes are for space research, voyages carrying humans into space have also accomplished a great deal on behalf of science. Since 1981, when the space shuttle *Columbia* was launched, astronauts have flown on nearly 130 shuttle missions. They have carried satellites into space, such as in July 2009 when a crew from the shuttle *Endeavor* deployed two satellites from the U.S. Naval Research Laboratory's ANDE 2 mission. Observing the satellites' respective orbits will allow researchers on the ground to study the density of Earth's atmosphere. Shuttle astronauts have also repaired malfunctioning satellites as well as made numerous repairs to the massive orbiting space telescope known as the Hubble.

One of the most significant accomplishments made by shuttle astronauts is helping to build the International Space Station (ISS). More than 15 countries are involved in its construction and occupancy, and it represents the world's largest international cooperative project. An orbiting scientific laboratory, the ISS is the biggest spacecraft that has ever been built. It is different from other types of spacecraft because of its primary focus: research performed *in* space, rather than research *about* space.

microgravity

A condition that results when an object is in free fall, creating a sense of weightlessness; low gravity.

Space station crew members spend much of their time conducting scientific experiments. This work makes use of microgravity, a condition that creates a sense of weightlessness. Microgravity presents the ideal environment for

Astronauts working in space with robotic arms and various tools have made numerous repairs to the orbiting Hubble Space Telescope (shown here in a computer illustration). Those repairs have enabled Hubble to send back unparalleled views from space.

experiments such as those that involve cell growth, because cells grow and multiply faster in space. Crew members have grown human cells to produce cultures that scientists on Earth can use to better understand the growth of tumors and how their growth might be controlled. Also, protein crystals grown in a microgravity environment are larger and purer than those grown on Earth. Crystals from ISS experiments help scientists learn more about the role proteins play in maintaining health and causing disease. Moreover, studies of the effects of microgravity on humans have expanded scientists' understanding of osteoporosis and balance disorders, and this has led to new treatments.

The Future Beckons

From the discovery of water on the moon to data gathered by robotic probes, space research has yielded a vast amount of information over the years. Scientists now know more about the universe, stars, and planets than ever before, and as this research continues, their scientific knowledge will continue to expand. Charles Bolden, who is a former astronaut and the administrator of NASA, is convinced that space research is invaluable, as he explains: "Through these missions, we will strengthen our nation's technological leadership and build strong international coalitions. The reasons for these new exploration missions are as old as the idea of America itself: discovery, science, innovation."[4]

What Is Space Research?

Humans have long been fascinated by the vast, mysterious universe, and it was this fascination that laid the foundation for space research. Over the years this research has broadened scientific knowledge about Earth's solar system, as well as produced a wealth of information about planets, galaxies, and stars in distant solar systems. Missions to asteroids and comets have revealed clues about how the universe formed and evolved over time, which helps scientists develop theories about Earth's origins. Moreover, space research has spawned numerous products and procedures that enhance science, technology, and medicine.

A September 2008 article by British physicist Stephen Hawking focused on the value of space research. Hawking referenced those who argue that money being spent on it would be better used to solve the problems of this planet, and he refuted that perspective with a historic analogy:

> In a way, the situation was like that in Europe before 1492. People might well have argued that it was a waste of money to send Columbus on a wild goose chase over an almost unimaginable distance. Yet, the discovery of the New World made a profound difference to the old one. Spreading out into space will have an even greater effect; it will completely change the future of the human race and maybe determine whether we have any future at all.[5]

Studying Solar Phenomena

Many scientists share Hawking's enthusiasm for space research, and they tout the innumerable discoveries that have been made because of it. One major focus of this research is the sun, because even though much has been learned about it over the years, a great deal remains unknown. Of considerable interest to scientists is space weather, which refers to all the

Comet Hale-Bopp streaks across the sky high over Joshua Tree National Park in California in March of 1997. Missions to comets and asteroids have revealed clues about how the universe formed.

cosmic disturbances caused by the sun's dynamic behavior. Two examples of space weather are sunspots, which are magnetic disturbances that appear as dark blotches on the sun, and solar flares, which are sudden eruptions of intense high-energy radiation on the sun's surface. Another element of space weather is solar wind, which blows at speeds of up to 2 million miles per hour (3.2 million kph) and is composed of electrically charged particles. By learning more about the changing nature of space weather, scientists can more accurately predict its potential impact on Earth.

Space tornadoes are an example of some of the most extreme space weather. Like tornadoes on Earth that are towers of violent, churning winds, space tornadoes are enormous funnel-shaped solar windstorms. They carry powerful electrical currents and roar through space at more than 1 million miles per hour (1.6 million kph). Space tornadoes form when solar wind hits Earth's magnetic field, wraps around it, and then stretches the field into a tail extending away from the sun. According to astrophysicist Andreas Keiling, it is much like "a rubber band being stretched and snapped back again. This creates lots of turbulence and forms the tornado."[6]

As puzzling as space tornadoes have been to scientists, NASA announced in April 2009 that some crucial questions about them had been answered. The mission, known as Time History of Events and Macroscale Interactions during Substorms, or THEMIS, involves 5 identical

⚛ A Rocket Pioneer

When physicist Robert H. Goddard first theorized that rockets powered by liquid fuels would have the capability of exploring the upper atmosphere and eventually the moon, he was ridiculed. A scathing editorial in the January 13, 1920, *New York Times* questioned his credentials as a scientist, saying his knowledge was akin to that of a high school science student. Goddard was furious, and he became secretive and reclusive. But the negative publicity did not stop him from continuing his work on rocket designs, and on March 16, 1926, he made history. He successfully launched the world's first liquid-propelled rocket, nicknamed Nell. Although it only rose 41 feet (12.5m) and flew for just 2.5 seconds, the world paid attention. Goddard had accomplished what no other scientist had and, in doing so, ushered in the modern rocket age.

By 1940 Goddard had developed more advanced rockets at his laboratory in Roswell, New Mexico. They grew bigger, became faster, and achieved greater and greater heights. Then in 1969, when the United States sent two astronauts to the moon, Goddard's prediction came true. He did not live to see this historic feat because he had died in 1945. But he would most certainly be honored at being named the father of modern rocketry.

spacecraft that are each about the size of a washing machine. Using data provided by the spacecraft, Keiling and a team of scientists were able to make the first precise, detailed measurements of space tornadoes. Among their observations was that the storms are created about once every 3 hours, and they are monsters— up to 44,000 miles (70,000km) long, which is enough to circle the Earth more than 1½ times.

The study also confirmed that solar tornadoes spark breathtaking displays of glowing colors in the sky called auroras, more commonly referred to as northern or southern lights. Auroras occur when electrons inside the space tornadoes collide with particles in the upper atmosphere, causing a burst of energy that makes molecules glow

Two interstellar tornadoes, captured by the Hubble Space Telescope 5,000 light years from Earth, spawn a brilliant display of colors. The violent, churning winds of these tornadoes roar through space at more than 1 million miles per hour.

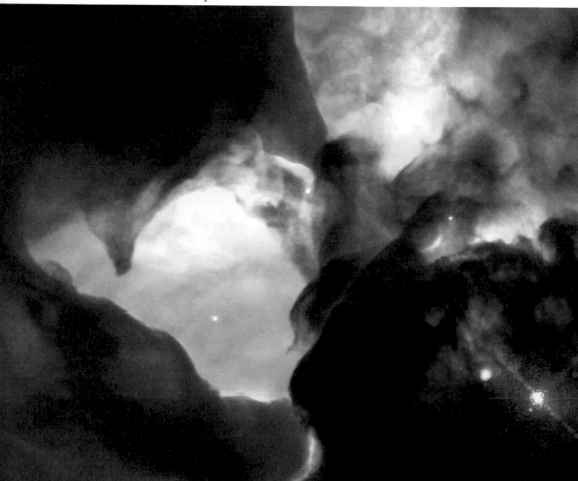

in bands of red, blue, and green light. In December 2009 THEMIS's network of cameras around the Arctic captured a northern lights phenomenon that scientists had never seen before. NASA says that the images showed "vast curtains" of auroras crashing together over and over, which produced "spectacular outbursts of light."[7]

Earth's Sister Planet

While missions such as THEMIS focus on solar phenomena, others are gathering information about the planets in Earth's solar system and beyond. A major priority is Mars, because by learning more about it, scientists hope to gain a better understanding of Earth's past and future. Research has suggested that about 4 billion years ago, when both planets formed, they may have been nearly identical. Even though Mars went through radical changes over time, it is still more like Earth than any other planet.

For instance, Mars and Earth are terrestrial planets, meaning they are rocky rather than gaseous. Both have mountains and valleys, weather and seasons, volcanoes and ice caps. At 24 hours and 39 minutes, the Martian day is only slightly longer than Earth's. Unlike Earth, however, the Martian climate is hostile, with extreme variations in temperature and such high concentrations of carbon dioxide in the atmosphere that it is poisonous for living things to breathe. Mars is not able to support life—but scientists say that it may not have always been that way.

terrestrial

Refers to a rocky surface, such as the terrestrial planets Earth, Mercury, Mars, and Venus.

In 2008 data from NASA's Mars Reconnaissance Orbiter showed that water once flowed freely on the Martian surface. Those who studied the data concluded that there had likely been large lakes, flowing rivers, and other wet environments on the planet. Over billions of years, as the climate and atmosphere changed, the water disappeared, which is mysterious to scientists. As a NASA article states:

What caused the change in Mars' climate? Were the conditions necessary for life to originate ever present on Mars? Could there be bacteria in the subsurface alive today? These are the questions that lead us to explore Mars. . . . By studying the reasons for climate change on Mars, which lacks the complications of oceans, a biosphere, and industrial contaminants, we may begin to understand the forces driving climate change on Earth. As we begin to explore the universe and search for planets in other solar systems, we must first ask the question "Did life occur on another planet in our own solar system?" and "What are the minimal conditions necessary for the formation of life?"[8]

Life in Deep Space?

Whether life once existed on Mars is intriguing to scientists, yet it is not the only planet they are curious about. Other, more distant planets may have harbored life as well—and whether some still might is one of the great mysteries of space research. This possibility came to light in April 2007, when Swiss scientists announced the discovery of the most Earth-like planet that had ever been found. The planet, known as Gliese 581 c is located trillions of miles away from Earth, and it orbits a star in the constellation Libra.

To study the planet, scientists used a spectrograph, a highly sophisticated instrument that takes measurements of a planet's relationship to its star. From the data gathered, the scientists were able to estimate that Gliese 581 c is about 50 percent larger than Earth, and its surface temperature is between 32°F and 104°F (0°C and 40°C). With such a hospitable climate, it is very possible that water exists on the planet—and if that is the case, life may exist there as well. Lead researcher Stephane Udry explains: "This means water can exist in liquid form. If you want life like our own, then you need water."[9] He adds that the newfound planet will likely become a target for future space missions that are searching for extraterrestrial life: "We still have a long way to go before reaching that point. But for sure it's the best candidate we know of right now."[10]

Monitoring Earth's Atmosphere

The possibility of life on other planets is exciting to many scientists, as Stanford University professor G. Scott Hubbard explains: "Exploration of space will provide humanity with an answer to the most fundamental questions: Are we alone? Are there other forms of life besides those on Earth?"[11] Yet searching for life elsewhere in space is only one focus of space research. For instance, the thousands of satellites currently in orbit around Earth capture information about stars and planets, as well as

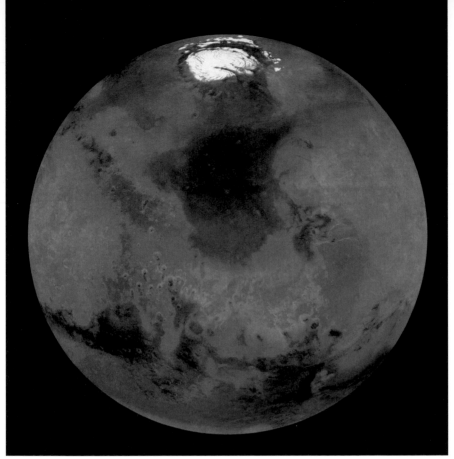

Scientists have studied Mars in hopes of gaining a better understanding of Earth's past and future. Both planets have mountains and valleys, weather and seasons, and volcanoes and ice caps. The north polar cap is visible at the top of this Mars photograph.

study phenomena that directly affect Earth. NASA's Cloud-Aerosol Lidar and Infrared Pathfinder Satellite Observation satellite, better known as CALIPSO, is outfitted with high-tech equipment such as a sophisticated light detection and ranging system. These instruments are providing scientists with new insight into the role that clouds and airborne particles called aerosols play in regulating Earth's weather, climate, and air quality.

In March 2009 NASA announced that CALIPSO had made a significant discovery about smoke in the atmosphere being generated by wildfires in Australia. Unlike most other satellites that cannot distinguish plumes of smoke from clouds, CALIPSO's instruments are hypersensitive and extremely powerful. Mike Fromm, who is a scientist with the U.S. Naval Research Laboratory in Washington, D.C., explains why this is important: "For the most part, smoke particles are smaller than cloud

Space Junk

At the same time probes and other spacecraft are orbiting the Earth, thousands of hunks of trash are doing the same. Known as space debris or space junk, the items may be anything from tools accidentally dropped by astronauts during spacewalks to parts and pieces that have broken off rockets or space shuttles. Satellites that are no longer functioning are also considered space junk. Because this orbiting trash dump is outside the atmosphere, it poses little risk to Earth. But it presents a potentially dangerous situation for astronauts in space and the vehicles that carry them there—especially because the debris is zooming through space at more than 9,300 miles per hour (15,000kph).

In September 2009 scientists at NASA spotted an old rocket part about 15 feet (5m) around that looked to be heading toward the International Space Station. They issued a warning to crew members, but then saw that the flying object was not as close as they had believed. The closest it came to the spacecraft was approximately the same distance as 14 football fields.

particles, and they have a shape that differs from ice crystals and water droplets. CALIPSO recognizes this and is able to distinguish smoke from clouds."[12] By observing the smoke, CALIPSO could clearly see that it was billowing up at a height of about 12 miles (19km), which scientists say is unusually high for a smoke plume.

CALIPSO's instruments also recorded that as the smoke continued to rise, aerosol particles were rapidly being dispersed into the atmosphere. This sort of information is valuable to scientists because it can help them learn more about how aerosols may affect global warming and/or cooling, as well as their role in influencing weather patterns. For instance, as the heat from a massive wildfire rises higher and higher, it can lead to a meteorological phenomenon known as a convective weather system, which refers to warmer molecules rising while cooler molecules sink. NASA's Jennifer Collings explains:

> Within this, a severe thunderstorm . . . develops. As the fire increases in strength, it acts like a chimney as it sucks the smoke from the flames up into the convective column. The smoke is

then injected into the atmosphere at abnormally high altitudes—a side effect similar to volcanic eruptions.[13]

Scientists say the effect of these events is a storm with greater intensity. CALIPSO continues to help researchers gain an understanding of the meteorological, chemical, and physical characteristics created by forest fires.

Clues Within Space Rocks

Another high priority of space research is the study of asteroids. Most of these rocky objects reside in the asteroid belt, a vast doughnut-shaped ring that is found between the orbits of Mars and Jupiter. Asteroids are ancient remnants of the solar system's formation, so when scientists study them it is akin to traveling billions of years back in time. They are believed to have formed during the same period and in similar environments as the bodies that evolved into terrestrial planets, which means they contain clues that reveal the conditions and processes that existed when the solar system was still very young. By analyzing the composition of asteroids, scientists hope to learn more about how Earth and other rocky planets originally formed. "In many ways," says NASA's Christopher Russell, "the asteroid belt is the leftovers from the Lego set used to build planets like Earth, Venus, Mars and Mercury. So we can take a deeper look at [the asteroids] Ceres and Vesta and ask, 'Do we need, say, three Vestas and two Ceres to make an Earth, or seven Ceres and two Vestas?' and so on."[14]

Asteroids range from tiny specks no bigger than a grain of sand to the size of enormous mountains. According to NASA, more than 200 known asteroids are larger than 60 miles (100km) in diameter, and some are far more massive. Kleopatra, for instance, is an asteroid that is shaped like a gigantic dog bone. It measures an estimated 135 miles (217km) long and 58 miles (94km) wide—about the same size as New Jersey. Scientists closely track the movement of asteroids, especially the largest ones, to assess the risk of one striking Earth—which could be disastrous, depending on the size of the asteroid and where it hit. This actually happened on June 30, 1908, in a remote area of Siberia known as Tunguska.

Early in the morning, startled witnesses watched as a fireball streaked through the sky, and then an asteroid weighing an estimated 220 million pounds (100 million kg) blew apart in a massive fiery blast. The explosion destroyed 800 square miles (2,100 sq. km) of forest and knocked over millions of trees. Very few people lived in the sparsely populated region so no one was killed. But had the asteroid hit the middle of a major city, the loss of human life would likely have been catastrophic. According to scientists, it is not a matter of *if* such a strike could happen again, but rather *when*, which is why they keep a careful, constant watch of asteroids.

Scientists monitor asteroids in various ways. For instance, NASA's Near Earth Object Observation Program, commonly called Spaceguard, plots the orbits of asteroids to determine if any could be potentially hazardous to Earth. One of the asteroids that astronomers are watching closely is called 2007 VK184, which is 430 feet (130m) in

The orbiting satellite CALIPSO (pictured in this computer illustration) aids scientists who are studying the role of clouds and aerosols in regulating Earth's weather, climate, and air quality.

diameter and has about a 1 in 3,000 chance of hitting Earth in 2048. An even bigger potential threat is Apophis because it is more than twice as big, and it is expected to swing uncomfortably close to Earth in the year 2029. Astronomer Robert Holmes explains: "It is going to pass so close it will come between the Earth and the satellites you get DirectTV off of."[15] Astronomers make these projections by scanning the sky for moving smudges of light that could indicate the presence of asteroids. Then they perform mathematical equations to calculate their orbits, evaluate the trajectories (flight paths) the asteroids are following, and make predictions about when or if they might be headed on a collision course with Earth.

Space Research Spinoffs

Because space research has yielded such an impressive amount of scientific information, new discoveries about the universe often garner the greatest amount of media attention. But space research has also resulted in numerous products and techniques that directly benefit people on Earth. Joan Vernikos, the former director of NASA's Life Sciences Division, explains: "The demanding technology of space compelled us to push the limits of human science and engineering achievements which, in turn, is pushing technology on Earth further. Without the innovation that spaceflight demands, we would not have this technology."[16] One example is a technique developed by NASA for protecting spacesuit visors from scratching and from the glare of the sun. It involves the application of a thin coat of polymer film. The optical company Foster Grant adopted the method and began using it in the manufacture of eyeglasses. "Now," writes Vernikos, "every pair of eyeglasses in the world is dipped in such a protective coating."[17]

polymer

Any of numerous natural and synthetic compounds of usually high molecular weight consisting of up to millions of repeated linked units, each a relatively light and simple molecule.

Vernikos also credits space research for the development of telemedicine, whereby medical information is transferred over the Internet. Initially developed as a way for NASA to monitor the health of astronauts in space, telemedicine now enables health-care practitioners in isolated communities and remote regions to consult with medical experts who are located far away, even in other countries. According to James Geiger, who is an anesthesiologist from Arizona, telemedicine has improved health care for people "in underserved areas of the world." He adds that this technology has led to "rapidly expanding methods of diagnosis and treatment,"[18] and it allows physicians to remotely monitor patients in hospitals worldwide. Critical care specialists and surgeons can use telemedicine to monitor vital signs of critically ill patients who may be in hospitals thousands of miles away. Geiger writes: "Healthcare in the 21st century is facing challenges digitally head-on."[19]

Also attributed to space research technology are a number of life-saving devices. For instance, NASA developed a line of polymer textiles that are used in spacesuits to protect astronauts from extreme temperatures in space. The same heat- and flame-resistant fiber is now used in suits for firefighters, people in military combat zones, and racecar drivers. Spacesuit technology also evolved into suits for professional deep-sea divers who are called to work in dangerous conditions. The suits protect the divers from extremely high-pressure environments in the ocean, toxic chemicals that are spilled in water from shipwrecks, and chemical and biological warfare agents. And in the event of biological threats, NASA technology has led to the development of a water analyzer. It can detect potential hazards in water used for agriculture, drinking, bathing, and at beaches and lakes, and it can alert authorities of those threats in a fraction of the time of conventional laboratory methods.

"It's Just the Beginning"

Whether it involves utilizing sophisticated technology to benefit human lives, gaining information about solar weather, or using data from Mars and asteroids to better understand Earth, space research has proved to be invaluable. In the coming years scientific knowledge will continue to expand, and exciting new discoveries will undoubtedly be made. Vernikos writes: "A whole new and exciting world of exploration lies ahead."[20]

Scientists worldwide are enthusiastic about what the future of space research may hold, and no one is more passionate about it than retired astronaut John Glenn. The pilot of America's first orbital flight in 1962, Glenn says that space research is vital because of all that it has accomplished in the past and all that it will continue to accomplish. He explains: "The last 50 years of the space program has been amazing, the number of developments in our whole society. It's just the beginning. . . . The research on materials and food and medicines that can be done up there is something that is vital to the future." Glenn adds that the benefits of space exploration far outweigh the cost: "The expense of doing it is so tiny. Economists have estimated that the money spent on NASA and research comes back about 10-to-1 in benefit. We can't just preserve all the old things. We have to continually be discovering the new."[21]

Probing the Universe

I n January 2008, after a journey through space that took nearly 4 years, a spacecraft called *MESSENGER* neared its destination: Mercury. The tiniest planet in Earth's solar system and the closest to the sun, Mercury is a terrestrial planet like Earth, Venus, and Mars. It is the densest of all planets, has the oldest surface, and has almost no atmosphere. Yet with all that is known about Mercury, the planet is still mysterious because it is the least explored of all the planets in Earth's solar system. Prior to *MESSENGER* only one probe had explored Mercury, NASA's *Mariner 10*, which visited the planet in the 1970s. The probe was able to examine and photograph less than half the planet, and the goal for *MESSENGER* is to cover much more territory and provide more in-depth information. NASA explains why this is important: "Understanding Mercury, and the forces that have shaped it, is fundamental to understanding the terrestrial planets and their evolution."[22]

As of May 2010 *MESSENGER* had completed three flybys and had photographed nearly 90 percent of Mercury's surface. The purpose of the flybys was for the spacecraft to get close enough that it could gain momentum from the planet's gravitational field, which is necessary in order for *MESSENGER* to enter its orbit. When that happens in 2011, the spacecraft will spend a year orbiting Mercury and in the process obtain answers to questions that have long puzzled scientists. Sean Solomon, principal investigator at the Carnegie Institution in Washington, D.C., shares his excitement about the mission. "As enticing as these flybys have been for discovering some of Mercury's secrets, they are the *hors d'oeuvres* to the mission's main course—observing Mercury from orbit for an entire year."[23]

Robots Hard at Work

Scientists value probes such as *MESSENGER* because of all the information their high-tech instruments can collect and transmit back to Earth. These spacecraft come in many different sizes and shapes, and what they are designed to accomplish differs according to the goals of the individual mission. One thing they all have in common is that they do not carry humans, but, rather, are robotic spacecraft that are controlled by scientists on Earth. This is a tremendous advantage over manned spacecraft because probes travel on journeys that often take years and cover millions, or even billions, of miles. No spacecraft exists that could safety enable humans to cover such long distances and spend such extraordinary amounts of time traveling in space.

Most probes are "disposable" spacecraft, meaning they are designed to accomplish their work and never return to Earth. The *Pioneer 10*, for example, was launched by NASA in 1972. It was the first spacecraft to travel through the asteroid belt, the first to make direct observations and obtain close-up images of Jupiter, and the first human-made object to leave the solar system and travel on a trajectory into interstellar space. The probe continued exploring for more than 30 years before NASA received its final, very weak signal on January 23, 2003. At the end of the mission *Pioneer 10* was more than 7.6 billion miles (12 billion km) away from Earth.

A Probe That Made History

Probes such as *Pioneer 10* and *MESSENGER* perform their work while in orbit, while others are designed to land on the surface of planets or moons. One example is the *Huygens* probe, which was a joint project of NASA and the European Space Agency. On January 14, 2010, scientists from the two agencies celebrated the 5-year anniversary of a historic event: the first time a probe landed on a celestial body in the outer solar system. *Huygens* traveled to Saturn on a spacecraft named *Cassini*, a journey that covered about 2 billion miles (3.2 billion km) and took nearly 7 years. Once it arrived, the probe separated from the spacecraft and parachuted down toward the surface of a moon called Titan.

On its way through Titan's thick atmosphere, *Huygens* took measurements of its composition, temperature, pressure, and wind speed, as well as snapped numerous photographs of the moon's surface. The Planetary Society describes scientists' reactions when they saw the images: "Before Cassini-Huygens' arrival, we could only imagine what the surface of Titan looked like. . . . The view of Titan revealed by Huygens' camera was astonishing: the landscape contained steep mountains dissected by river-cut valleys surrounded by dry lakebeds, much like the landscape of an Earth desert."[24] One of the probe's instruments poked into the ground and found that Titan's soil had the consistency of wet sand or clay and was covered by a thin crust.

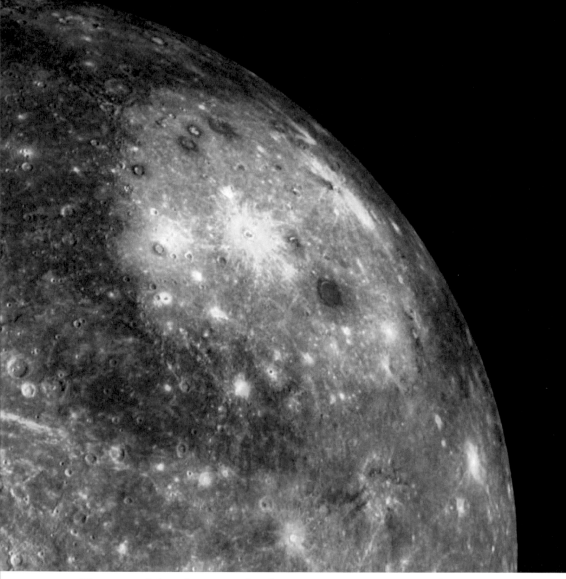

The 2008 flyby of Mercury by the MESSENGER *spacecraft gave support to the theory that volcanic activity formed the planet's many smooth, flat plains. In this color-enhanced image of Mercury, taken by* MESSENGER, *scientists identified signs of extinct volcanoes in several of the bright orange regions.*

Although *Huygens* only transmitted data for a few hours after landing, the probe lasted longer than its creators had envisioned. Moreover, the data that it transmitted answered many questions that scientists had wondered about for years, and this heightened their interest in further studies of Saturn's moon. Jean-Pierre Lebreton, Huygens project scientist for the European Space Agency, explains: "The Huygens mission was the most spectacular success, as shown by . . . the fact that we are still extracting new information from the data. We will continue to use these data to understand more and more about Titan for many years to come, and transmit all that we know—and don't know—to future Titan explorers."[25]

Roving Robots

The Mars Exploration Rover mission also involved probes landing and sending data back to Earth. The difference, though, is that this mission involves robots that not only landed on the surface of Mars, they travel around and explore the planet. Launched by the United States in June 2003, 2 Mars Exploration Rover spacecraft carrying the rovers *Spirit* and *Opportunity* traveled for nearly 7 months and covered 64 million miles (103 million km) on the journey to Mars. The spacecraft, each of which was encased in a massive cluster of protective airbags, hit the Martian surface in 2 different locations. They bounced high in the air several times, then rolled to a stop and opened up the doors. *Spirit* and *Opportunity* rolled out and immediately began exploring and transmitting data back to Earth-based scientists.

Although NASA anticipated only a three-month life span for the robots, they far surpassed expectations by remaining operational for more than six years. As of May 2010 *Opportunity* was still roaming around the Martian surface. *Spirit* was stuck in deep sand and could not move, but the robot was still able to communicate with ground controllers. During their time on Mars, *Spirit* and *Opportunity* have climbed mountains, descended into craters, surveyed impact damage from meteorites, and traveled through raging dust storms, for which the red planet is well known. According to NASA, the rovers have made numerous important discoveries. Together they have returned a quarter-million photographs and transmitted more than 36 gigabytes of data. This information helps scientists learn more about Mars's ancient past, which they hope will increase their understanding of why the planet changed so drastically during its history.

Clues from Ancient Ice Balls

Another probe that is expected to provide clues about the ancient past is known as *Deep Impact*, which will study comets. Launched in January 2005, *Deep Impact* will be the first spacecraft to probe beneath the surface of a comet to reveal the secrets of its interior composition. NASA calls comets "time capsules" because they are composed of primitive debris from the coldest and most distant regions of the solar system. By studying them, scientists hope to learn more about how the solar system formed and evolved over time.

Deep Impact arrived at its first destination, a comet known as Tempel 1, nearly 6 months after launch and began using its sophisticated cameras to collect images. Then it released a separate "impactor" spacecraft, which slammed into the comet at a speed of 23,000 miles per hour (37,000kph). The collision blasted open a massive crater and shot a towering plume of debris upward and outward from the comet. To analyze the composition of the billowing cloud, the orbiting spacecraft used spectrometers, which use light or radiation to identify the chemical makeup of a material. After examining the data, scientists learned that the cloud was made up of very fine, powdery material that was held together by gravity.

spectrometer

A device that uses light or radiation to identify the chemical makeup of a material.

According to NASA officials, the *Deep Impact* mission has yielded crucial information about the structure and composition of comets. For instance, scientists have long known that a major component in comets is water ice, but they were unsure whether the ice was mainly inside or could also be found on the surface. *Deep Impact* confirmed that the latter was true when it found signs of water ice on Tempel 1's surface. Another finding was that the comet's interior is well shielded from the solar rays that heat its surface. NASA explains the significance of this: "Mission data indicate the nucleus is extremely porous, allowing the surface to heat up and cool down almost instantly in response to sunlight. This suggests heat is not easily conducted to the interior, and the ice and other material deep inside the nucleus may be pristine and unchanged from the early days of the solar system, just as many scientists had suggested."[26]

After the Tempel 1 mission was completed, NASA officials planned to send the *Deep Impact* probe to explore a comet named Boethin. But as astronomers throughout the world scoured the skies looking for it, the comet appeared to have vanished. So mission controllers changed the probe's trajectory to head it toward a comet named Hartley 2. When it reaches the comet in November 2010, the spacecraft will utilize the same

A Woman of Many "Firsts"

As a child growing up in Elmira, New York, in the 1960s and 1970s Eileen Collins was fascinated by stories of space, yet she could not help wondering why there were no female astronauts. She was inspired by NASA's first missions, and when she was in college she found that new opportunities were opening up for women in aviation. After graduation she became one of the first women to go straight from college into the U.S. Air Force's pilot training program. Soon afterward her base was visited by the newest astronaut class, which was the first to admit women. At that point there was no doubt in her mind that she wanted to be one of them.

In 1990 Collins was selected by NASA for its training program, and 18 months later she became an astronaut—one who went on to make history. During a 1995 mission to the Russian space station Mir, Collins became the first woman to pilot the space shuttle. Four years later, she earned the distinction of being the first female commander of a shuttle mission.

suite of scientific instruments as it used to analyze Tempel 1. Again, its goal will be to further increase scientific understanding of the composition of comets.

A Journey into the Past

Gathering data about the solar system's ancient past is also the goal of a spacecraft known as *Dawn*, but it will analyze asteroids rather than comets. Launched in September 2007, the spacecraft will spend at least 8 years covering a distance of more than 3.2 billion miles (5.1 billion km). On November 13, 2009, *Dawn* entered the main asteroid belt between the orbits of Mars and Jupiter, but its journey was far from over. The probe's destination is an asteroid known as Vesta, which it will not reach until July 2011. After its Vesta mission is complete, *Dawn* will fly to the asteroid Ceres and is expected to arrive there sometime during 2015. NASA states that Vesta and Ceres were chosen because, unlike many other asteroids, these 2 monstrous space rocks somehow managed to survive the hostile, violent collisions that once shook the universe. Although scientists have no idea why, both asteroids have remained intact since their formation.

During its lengthy journey, *Dawn* will utilize sophisticated instruments such as spectrometers to identify the asteroids' surface minerals. Another instrument, called a gamma ray and neutron spectrometer, will determine the elements that make up the outer parts of the asteroids. Scientific equipment will also allow the *Dawn* spacecraft to measure the gravity field around the asteroids, thereby revealing details about their interior composition. NASA writes:

> With the data from these systems, scientists will study surface features and the complex and varied landscapes, gaining valuable new insights into the internal structure of these ancient worlds. What role did size have in determining how planets evolved throughout the Solar System? How did water affect the process of planetary formation? Data gathered during the Dawn mission will help scientists uncover the answers to these and other questions.[27]

Solar Storms and Space Weather

As the *Dawn* spacecraft zooms through space on its long journey to Vesta and Ceres, the Solar Terrestrial Relations Observatory (STEREO) is studying the sun. Earth's star is mysterious to scientists in many ways, but in 2009 STEREO solved one of its greatest mysteries—phenomena known as solar tsunamis are indeed real. Twin STEREO probes recorded a coronal mass ejection (CME), which is a violent solar explosion. CMEs are powerful enough to blow as much as 10 billion tons (9.8 billion metric tons) of the sun's atmosphere into interplanetary space at speeds of about 1 million miles per hour (1.6 million kph). Much like underwater earthquakes trigger tsunamis in the ocean, the blast observed by the STEREO probes caused a massive wave of hot plasma and magnetism to roar across the surface of the sun at 560,000 miles per hour (901,000kph). And a team of astounded scientists watched it happen.

coronal mass ejection

A violent solar explosion during which a huge cloud of hot plasma is expelled from the sun.

This was not the first time that tsunami-like waves had been seen on the sun. They were originally observed in 1997, when scientists examined images transmitted by the *Solar and Heliospheric Observatory*

(*SOHO*) spacecraft. At the time, many were skeptical that such a phenomenon was possible, and they wondered if they were mistaken. In fact, according to NASA's Tony Phillips, the scientists "doubted their senses." He explains: "The scale of the thing was staggering. It rose up higher than Earth itself and rippled out from a central point in a circular pattern millions of kilometers in circumference. Skeptical observers suggested it might be a shadow of some kind—a trick of the eye—but surely not a real wave."[28] STEREO, however, proved the scientists wrong.

Unlike *SOHO*'s two-dimensional images, the STEREO probes were able to produce unprecedented three-dimensional images of the sun. This is because of the probes' unique positioning, whereby they are offset from each other and Earth. One probe is orbiting ahead of Earth, and the other lags behind as Earth orbits the sun. NASA explains why this is so effective: "Just as the slight offset between eyes provides depth perception, this placement will allow the STEREO observatories to obtain 3-D images of the sun."[29]

The STEREO probes have provided an unparalleled scientific tool for studying solar tsunamis and other phenomena. Each spacecraft is outfitted with 16 different instruments, including imaging telescopes and other highly sophisticated equipment. An article on the Science Daily Web site explains how these instruments help scientists study solar activity:

> **solar tsunami**
>
> A massive wave of hot plasma and magnetism that roars across the surface of the sun.

> Using three-dimensional observations, solar physicists can examine a CME's structure, velocity, mass, and direction in the corona [the sun's outer atmospheric layer] while tracking it through interplanetary space. These measurements can help determine when a CME will reach Earth and predict how much energy it will deliver to our magnetosphere, which is Earth's protective magnetic shield.[30]

Studying CMEs allows scientists to monitor the sun closely and gauge its relationship to space weather, which can affect Earth in a number of ways. For example, when solar cosmic rays plow into Earth's atmosphere, this can create auroras. But the effects of solar weather can also be highly destructive because it disrupts Earth's electromagnetic fields. The result can be powerful surges that overload electrical wires and lead to widespread blackouts. Another hazardous effect of space weather is its potential interference with communication between ground engineers and satellites, as well as between air traffic control operations and airplanes.

Space weather can also be extremely dangerous for astronauts who are performing spacewalks outside the protection of the International Space Station. Another risk is that it can damage or even destroy satellites and other spacecraft in orbit. Scientists' hope for STEREO is that it will provide enough information about solar weather that they will eventually be able to forecast it, much like meteorological technology helps predict Earth's weather.

Mapping the Solar System

A probe known as the Interstellar Boundary Explorer (IBEX) is also studying solar phenomena and scouring the universe—even though it is no bigger than a bus tire. Launched in October 2008, one of its objectives is to better define the interaction between the solar wind and the interstellar boundary, a region where hot solar wind slams into the cold expanse of space. This interactive process forms the heliosphere, which is the entire region of space that is influenced by the sun and its magnetic field. The heliosphere acts as a protective bubble around the solar system. David McComas, who is the principal investigator for the IBEX mission, explains the importance of this protection: "The interstellar boundary regions are critical because they shield us from the vast majority of dangerous galactic cosmic rays, which otherwise would penetrate into Earth's orbit and make human spaceflight much more dangerous."[31]

interstellar boundary

A region where hot solar wind slams into the cold expanse of space to form the heliosphere, which acts as a protective bubble for the solar system.

IBEX is outfitted with two sensors that are similar to telescopes, but instead of collecting light they collect particles known as energetic neutron atoms. The spacecraft was designed that way because the interstellar region is so far out in space that it emits no light, so conventional telescopes cannot see it. During its orbit IBEX continuously spins, which enables it to collect particles from every part of the sky. As these are gathered, the sensors and spacecraft keep track of where the particles came from, the time they entered the sensors, their mass, and the amount of energy each particle has. From particles that were collected over a period of six months, scientists have been able to construct the first comprehensive map of the solar system, including its location in the Milky Way galaxy. As McComas explains: "For the first time, we're sticking our heads out of the sun's atmosphere and beginning to really understand our place in the galaxy."[32]

Scientists have searched for years for signs of water on Mars. The odd-shaped lumpy rock (right), captured in this photograph by the Mars Exploration Rover Opportunity, *suggests the presence of water at some time in the planet's history. Scientists believe this and similar rocks may have formed when larger rocks dried and cracked after exposure to water.*

A Sand-Trapped Robot

For more than 6 years the rovers *Spirit* and *Opportunity* have been exploring Mars and have made many discoveries, including confirming that water once ran freely on the planet. *Spirit* has had a few problems along the way, such as in 2006 when 1 of its 6 wheels jammed. To overcome the glitch, mission controllers programmed the rover to drive backward, which it has done ever since. Then in 2009 *Spirit* found itself in another predicament when it became stuck in loose soil on the edge of a small crater. At first scientists were frustrated because the robot could not get free—then they realized that it was an advantage. As *Spirit* spun its wheels to free itself, it broke through the dark, crusty surface and churned up the soil underneath. As scientists analyzed the rover's data, they found that the soil contained minerals known as sulfates, which are known to have formed in ancient steam vents. This was exciting because it was yet one more sign of the presence of water, and it could indicate that such areas once supported life. According to scientist Ray Arvidson, this discovery would not have been made if *Spirit* had not gotten stuck.

McComas adds that the maps created from IBEX's data provide a new way for scientists to analyze Earth's place in the galaxy, and he says some of the findings have been surprising. He writes:

> The IBEX results are truly remarkable! What we are seeing in these maps does not match with any of the previous theoretical models of this region. It will be exciting for scientists to review these maps and revise the way we understand our heliosphere and how it interacts with the galaxy. Different conditions can create energetic neutron atoms, so the scientists' job now is to make new models based on these maps. They will provide a much better picture of how we are affected by our region of the Milky Way galaxy.[33]

According to NASA, one advantage of the new maps is their ability to help clarify the overall shape of the bubble, which could be affected by differences in density and magnetic fields in the interstellar region.

Decades of Progress

Over the years space probes have yielded an astonishing amount of information. They have proved that raging solar tsunamis actually do occur on the surface of the sun. Probes have also helped scientists better understand space weather and its potential threats to Earth. Studies of comets and asteroids are providing clues about the ancient past, such as how the universe evolved and how planets formed. The IBEX mission has enabled scientists to map Earth's solar system, which has increased their understanding of the interactions between solar wind and the Milky Way galaxy. As these robotic spacecraft continue to probe the universe, scientific knowledge will continue to expand, and more mysteries of the cosmos will undoubtedly be solved.

Living and Working in Space

In November 2009 NASA announced its intention to analyze environmental issues that affect Earth—from more than 200 miles (322km) above, at the International Space Station (ISS). The project's official name is Superconduction Submillimeter-wave Limb-emission Sounder, or SMILES for short. It is different from other ISS experiments because for the first time, the work will be conducted outside the station. This was made possible by the Japanese Aerospace Exploration Agency, which built a laboratory module known as Kibo, the Japanese word for *hope*, with an attached exterior platform where science experiments can be deployed and conducted in open space. Astronaut Dave Wolf explains how the platform enhances the ISS's capabilities: "It's a large external porch to the space station where high quality experiments can be conducted in the high vacuum of space. It's really an exceptionally valuable piece of real estate."[34]

> **stratosphere**
>
> The part of the earth's atmosphere that extends from about 7–31 miles (11–50k) above the surface, where temperatures gradually increase with altitude and clouds rarely form.

SMILES utilizes spectrometers, sensors, and other highly sophisticated instruments that measure gases such as chlorine and bromine in the atmosphere. High concentrations of these gases in an atmospheric region known as the stratosphere contribute to the depletion of the ozone layer, which protects Earth by absorbing much of the sun's harmful ultraviolet radiation. Scientists are excited about SMILES because the instruments used are able to measure minute traces of atmospheric gases that were previously too small to be detected. One observation showed that ozone concentrations were greater around Earth's equatorial region than at higher latitudes. This sort of information helps scientists better understand the characteristics of ozone distribution worldwide, including how it changes over time.

The World's Largest Spacecraft

The SMILES project is indicative of how the ISS has grown and evolved over the years. Initial planning for the space station began in the early 1990s when officials from the United States and Russia met to discuss building a large, orbiting laboratory where scientists could live and work for extended periods of time. Japan, Canada, Brazil, and countries in the European Union were also partners in the collaborative effort.

One aspect of the project that was clear at the outset was that unlike other types of spacecraft, the ISS could not be built on Earth and then launched into orbit—it is far too massive for that. As big as a football field (including the end zones) and weighing nearly 700,000 pounds (317,515kg), the ISS is the largest spacecraft that has ever been built. No rocket exists that is big enough or powerful enough to propel such an enormous object into orbit. Instead, individual components are designed and constructed on the ground and then carried into space by shuttles or Russian rockets. Then astronauts and cosmonauts assemble the ISS in space, one piece at a time. When it is complete, the ISS will include about 8 large cylindrical sections known as modules, with 8 massive solar panels that supply electrical power.

The first component of the ISS was launched by Russia in 1998. Known as Zarya, which is Russian for *sunrise*, the module initially performed as the heart of the space station by generating power and providing propulsion. Just over 2 weeks after Zarya was in place, astronauts flew on a space shuttle to the ISS with a module known as Unity, a name that was significant because it symbolized the joining of the Russian side to the American side. In July 2000, with the arrival of Russia's Zvezda service module, the ISS added living quarters, life support mechanisms, and environmental controls. The orbiting laboratory was finally ready for its first crew of 2 Russian cosmonauts and 1 American astronaut.

In the years following the initial construction of the ISS, more modules were furnished by Japan and members of the European Space Agency, as well as by Russia and the United States, and a huge robotic arm was donated by Canada. Astronauts and cosmonauts worked together to assemble the additional components and expand the size of the spacecraft. Former astronaut Bob Cabana, who is now director of NASA's Kennedy Space Center in Florida, shares his thoughts about the significance of this global partnership: "You take all those different cultures, people and hardware built around the world and it comes together for the first time on orbit and it works flawlessly—that's phenomenal."[35] As of May 2010 the ISS was not yet complete, but it had grown large enough to accommodate its planned capacity of six crew members.

Space Station Life

The ISS provides generous living and working quarters for its inhabitants, with as much interior space as a jumbo jet. There are 5 laboratories where crew members perform scientific experiments, as well as 5 bedrooms, 2 kitchens, 2 bathrooms, and ample room for exercise equipment. The ISS is so spacious, in fact, that in July 2009 a record-breaking total of 13 crew members were staying there, although they acknowledged that it was a bit crowded.

Astronauts and cosmonauts typically stay at the ISS for 4 to 6 months, and then leave when new crews arrive to replace them. Their days are highly structured, with specific amounts of time allotted for meals, housekeeping duties to keep the station clean, scientific experiments, spacewalks to assemble modules or make repairs, entertainment and socializing, exercising, and of course, sleeping—but that can be challenging. To keep from floating around during the night, most crew members zip themselves into sleeping bags that attach to walls with Velcro fasteners. Also, trying to sleep can be very difficult since the concepts of day and night are nothing like what people experience on Earth. For those on board the ISS, 16 sunrises occur every 24 hours as the spacecraft speeds along in its orbit around Earth. Because it is seldom dark, crew members often cover the windows to block out the brilliant sunlight.

The greatest challenge for many who reside on the ISS, at least at first, is becoming adjusted to the microgravity environment. Yet even though this can be challenging, crew members believe that the many scientific experiments made possible because of microgravity outweigh the inconvenience of coping with it. These experiments may be conducted by space station crew members or by scientists back on Earth. NASA's Steven Roy explains: "Today, scientists see their experiments launched into space and once the experiments are activated, scientists can control and collect data . . . from ground stations. Many experiments require direct astronaut involvement, but many do not, freeing

Space station astronauts zip themselves into sleeping bags that attach to the walls to keep from floating around during the night. Visiting shuttle astronauts do the same while docked at the space station.

the astronauts to perform their own science investigations and operate the station."[36] Roy estimates that the increase in planned laboratory space on the ISS will triple the number of hours dedicated to science in the next few years.

NASA states that experiments performed by ISS crew members have been invaluable in terms of scientific understanding and tangible benefits to humans. As the agency explains: "Advancing our knowledge in the areas of human physiology, biology, material and physical sciences, and translating that knowledge to health, socioeconomic, and environmental benefits on Earth is another common goal of the [ISS] agencies: returning the knowledge gained in space research for the benefit of society."[37] Research at the ISS covers a broad range of sciences, including human life sciences, biological science, human physiology, physical and materials science, and Earth and space science. To date, more than 400 experiments have been conducted on the ISS, with 100 to 150 in progress at any given time.

What Causes Microgravity?

Magazines and Web sites often display pictures of astronauts floating around inside the International Space Station, and many people think it is caused by a lack of gravity. That is not correct, however, as the gravity in orbit is only slightly weaker than the gravity on Earth's surface. The weightless feeling experienced by crew members is due to microgravity. When a spacecraft is in orbit, Earth's strong gravitational force is constantly pulling it toward the planet, which puts it in a state of free fall. This continuous falling seems to eliminate the weight of everyone and everything inside the spacecraft, which is why it is often called weightlessness.

So if the International Space Station is hurtling toward Earth, what keeps it from falling out of the sky? The answer is its tremendous speed of about 26,000 feet (7,900m) per second. As it falls, its horizontal speed is so fast that the Earth's surface curves away from it on a continuous basis. Thus, the spacecraft holds its position and continues to travel in a circular pattern.

Benefits to Human Health

Some of the most valuable studies aboard the ISS have involved analyzing the behavior of certain types of germs. *Salmonella*, for instance, is a genus of bacteria that is most commonly associated with food poisoning. During ISS experiments with a strain known as *Salmonella typhimurium*, scientists discovered that its virulence, meaning its strong potential to cause disease, markedly increased in the microgravity of the ISS. Following the discovery, experiments by researchers from Arizona State University showed that by changing the bacteria's growth environment, the

virulence

The strong potential of bacteria or viruses to cause disease.

pathogen's virulence could be controlled, or "switched off." Expansion of this research could potentially benefit people on Earth, as well as astronauts traveling in space. NASA scientist Julie Robinson explains: "This research opens up new areas for investigations that may improve food treatment, develop new therapies and vaccines to combat food poisoning in humans here on Earth, and protect astronauts on orbit from infectious disease."[38]

Another ISS experiment resulted in a breakthrough medical discovery: a new method of delivering drugs to targeted areas in the human body. During the Microencapsulation of Anti-tumor Drugs experiment, ISS scientists were able to develop "microballoons," or liquid-filled capsules that are roughly the same size as blood cells. According to NASA, the space station environment was vital for this project because in microgravity, the liquids and their outer balloon structures formed spontaneously.

Astronaut and scientist Peggy Whitson displays soybean plants grown aboard the International Space Station. Research on plant growth in reduced gravity is one of many experiments conducted on the space station and monitored by Earth-based scientists.

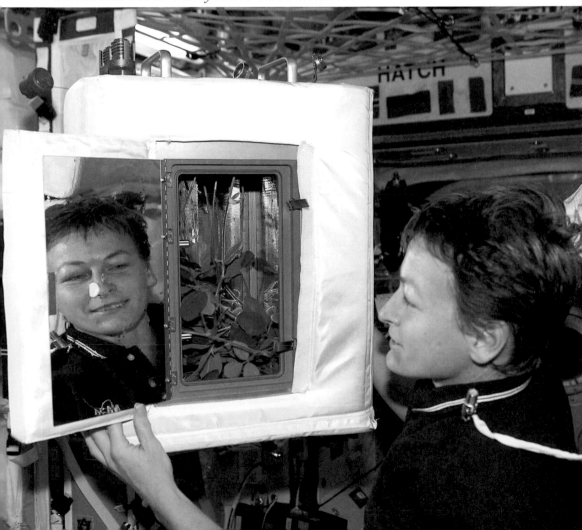

The use of microcapsules can benefit patients who suffer from a number of diseases, as NASA explains:

> For example, diabetes patients can use implanted microcapsules as treatment instead of daily insulin shots. Another . . . application of microcapsules is the delivery of drugs directly to cancer cells. This method can be used as a substitution for traditional anti-cancer treatments, such as chemotherapy, that involve large quantities of drugs that affect the entire body. The microcapsules contain a smaller dose of medication that directly targets tumors; smaller doses and targeted drug delivery help reduce the unwanted side effects that are currently produced by chemotherapy.[39]

The success of microcapsules was demonstrated in clinical trials involving cancer patients. When malignant tumors of the lung and prostate were treated with only a few injections, it inhibited the tumors' growth. Microcapsules have also been developed for treating deep-tissue infection and blood-clotting disorders.

Product Improvements

In addition to research that benefits medical science and improves human health, some experiments performed on the ISS could lead to better products on Earth. For instance, studies that are conducted in the space station's Materials Science Research Rack may help pave the way for the creation of improved metals and glass. A joint project of NASA and the European Space Agency, the research rack is a laboratory that is about the size of a large refrigerator. A September 2009 article states that the research rack "will provide hardware to control the thermal, environmental and vacuum conditions of experiments; monitor experiments with video; and supply power and data handling for specific experiment instrumentation."[40]

ISS crew members use the research rack to conduct experiments with a variety of materials such as metal, alloys, ceramics, polymers, and glass. This research will allow the scientists to see how the materials form, as well as learn how to control their properties. NASA scientist Sandor Lehoczky explains the benefit of the experiments: "The goal of materials processing in space is to develop a better understanding of how process-

ing affects materials properties without the complication of gravity causing density effects on the processes. With this knowledge, reliable predictions can be made about the conditions required on Earth to achieve
improved materials."[41]

Earth Observations

Along with performing experiments, those who reside on the ISS help
with research that supports Earth-based scientists. One ongoing project is known as Crew Earth Observations, or CEO, which involves

*The International Space Station offers a unique view of Australia's
Great Barrier Reef (pictured), home to more than 400 types of coral
and thousands of animal species. Scientists use photographs such as
this one to monitor environmental and geological changes.*

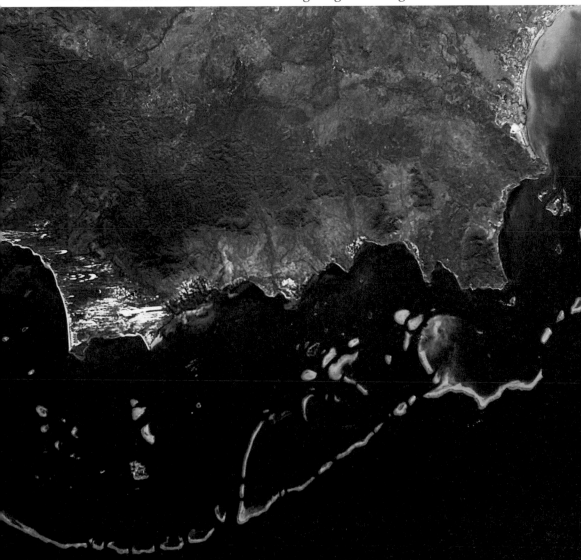

crew members photographing surface areas throughout the world. These photographs are used as educational and research tools, as well as adding to historical records of global environmental change, geological and weather events, and the growth and change of human-induced features such as cities. The ISS provides an exceptional venue for capturing sites and events on Earth because it makes repeated passes over the planet while astronauts use various lighting and viewing angles for their photographs.

The 2006 eruption of the Cleveland volcano in Alaska's Aleutian Island chain was captured on film by space station astronaut Jeff Williams.

Space Station Scare

When spacecraft are scheduled to dock with the International Space Station (ISS), its position in orbit sometimes needs to be changed. This is achieved by what is known as a rocket burn, whereby engines fire up under autopilot control and slightly boost the ISS upward. Usually this is a routine and uneventful occurrence involving such gentle movement that crew members barely notice it and can even sleep through it. But this was definitely not the case on January 14, 2009.

As soon as the engines started on that day, the massive array of solar wings began swaying and the station started to vibrate. Mounted equipment and cables flopped back and forth and objects were shaken loose from walls while a video camera, wildly swaying on its own mounting bracket, recorded the scene. More than two minutes passed before the alarming situation ended, and the three crew members floated through the station's cabin plucking loose items out of the air and reattaching them to the walls. A review found that an error in engine control settings was to blame.

Examples of photographs taken from the ISS include coral reefs; icebergs in the South Atlantic Ocean; alpine glaciers; Pacific Ocean atolls, which are islands that consist of a circular coral reef surrounding lagoons; and impact craters on Earth that closely resemble those on other planets. Also photographed are events such as floods and forest fires, the eruption of volcanoes, and damage from hurricanes, earthquakes, and tsunamis. In May 2006 ISS flight engineer Jeff Williams observed the eruption of the Cleveland volcano in Alaska's Aleutian Island chain. He could see that a massive plume of ash had formed above the volcano and was drifting away from its summit in a west-southwest direction, and he was the first to photograph it and report it to the Alaska Volcano Observatory. This was important information because ash plumes can present a hazard for jet flights.

As part of the CEO endeavor, ISS crew members studied and photographed Earth's polar regions from 2007 to 2009. Using still digital photography and video equipment, the crew captured images of polar phenomena such as sea ice, auroras, and cloud cover. A NASA fact sheet describes the relevance of such photographs: "Today, handheld photography of the world from human spaceflight missions, spanning more than 40 years, provides valuable insight into Earth processes and the effects of human activities on the planet."[42]

The information gleaned from space is often used in conjunction with data gathered from satellites and ground observatories to help scientists better understand the relationship between climate change and the polar regions. NASA explains the value of this: "ISS, as a platform for these observations, will contribute data that has not been available in the past and will set the precedent for future international scientific collaborations for Earth observations."[43] In January 2008 ISS crew members collaborated with researchers from the National Snow and Ice Data Center in Boulder, Colorado. The researchers requested space photographs of icebergs that had broken off from a major ice shelf in Antarctica. Once these images had been taken, they provided the first observations of melted water pooling on top of the icebergs as they disintegrated and drifted into the Atlantic Ocean. This will help scientists study the accelerated breakup of sea ice, which many believe is a sign of accelerated warming of the planet.

Strong Support for the Space Station

Because NASA has played such an important role in the planning, construction, and staffing of the ISS, many were stunned at an announcement that was made in June 2009. NASA officials stated that once the space station had been completed, it might be de-orbited in the first quarter of 2016. By "de-orbited," NASA meant that the ISS would be allowed to fall back into the atmosphere, burn up, and crash into the Pacific Ocean. Although no country owns the space station, NASA has made significant financial contributions to its construction, and the agency had not budgeted for operating expenses beyond the year 2015. Without support from the United States, other countries may not be able to afford the cost.

de-orbit

Allowing a spacecraft to fall back into the atmosphere and burn up.

Many scientists were extremely dismayed at the possibility of the United States abandoning the ISS. They cited the tens of billions of dollars spent on space station construction and operation as well as the invaluable research being done aboard it. Members of a committee appointed by the White House shared this perspective, and in a report issued in October 2009, the group recommended that the life of the ISS be extended to at least 2020. The authors wrote:

> It seems unwise to de-orbit the Station after . . . only five years of operational life. *Not* to extend its operation would significantly impair U.S. ability to develop and lead future international spaceflight partnerships. Further, the ISS should be funded to enable it to achieve its full potential: as the nation's newest national laboratory, as an enhanced test bed for technologies and operational techniques that support exploration, and as a framework that can support expanded international collaboration.[44]

After nearly a year of uncertainty about the space station's fate, its supporters welcomed an announcement by President Barack Obama on April 15, 2010. In a speech given at NASA's John F. Kennedy Space Center, Obama expressed his support for space research and hailed all that had been accomplished over the past decades. He also spoke about why it was crucial for the United States to forge ahead with space research:

> Because broadening our capabilities in space will continue to serve our society in ways that we can scarcely imagine. Because exploration will once more inspire wonder in a new generation—sparking passions and launching careers. And because, ultimately, if we fail to press forward in the pursuit of discovery, we are ceding our future and we are ceding that essential element of the American character.[45]

In his speech, Obama outlined his goals for the future of America's space research, and stated his intention to increase NASA's budget by $6 billion. He also announced that the life of the International Space Station would be extended to 2020 or beyond.

Looking Ahead

Scientists worldwide are excited about the research and discoveries that have taken place aboard the International Space Station. They also applaud the international collaboration that has made such work possible. With its life being extended for at least another decade, perhaps even greater feats will be accomplished in the future. Roy offers his thoughts:

> By any stretch of the imagination [the] space station has been an unqualified success in political, technological, engineering and scientific partnerships and is perhaps the greatest demonstration of peaceful human cooperation and achievement in history. It is a testimony to what humanity can achieve in unity of purpose and peace; and a testimony to the role of space travel to bring together diverse peoples for common good.[46]

Eyes on the Universe

On the morning of July 20, 2009, astronomers at Hawaii's Keck Observatory were keeping a close watch on the sky. They could see something that had only been observed once before—the aftermath of a comet or other space object that had slammed into Jupiter. An amateur astronomer from Australia was the first to spot the mysterious black smudge on the planet, and he alerted other scientists about it. Although astronomers estimated that the object was no more than 1 mile (1.6km) across, it was obviously traveling at an exorbitant rate of speed. The object exploded as it plowed through Jupiter's thick atmosphere, blasting open a monstrous hole as big as the Earth.

This phenomenon was interesting to scientists because they previously believed that such collisions occurred only once every few thousand years, and this strike was the second in 15 years. According to physicist Michio Kaku, the event could prove to be a warning for people on Earth. He writes:

> Perhaps Mother Nature was just trying to show what little scientists really understand about these cosmic collisions.
>
> . . . Maybe Mother Nature was reminding us that the universe is, after all, a violent place? . . . The earth lies in the middle of a cosmic shooting gallery. The proof comes out every night when we gaze at the moon.
>
> When viewing the film of Neil Armstrong and Buzz Aldrin bobbing among the barren craters of the Moon, we are reminded that each crater was gouged out by a titanic impact.[47]

Amazing Observations

Discoveries such as the Jupiter collision have been possible because of powerful telescopes, which allow scientists to observe planets and galaxies that are billions or even trillions of miles away. These celestial bodies are so distant, in fact, that astronomers do not use miles or kilometers when referring to their location in the universe. Instead they use the term *light-year*, which is a measure of the distance that light can travel in a year. One light-year is equivalent to nearly 6 trillion miles (9.6 trillion km). To put the vast expanse of space into perspective, Proxima Centauri, Earth's second-closest star after the sun, is 4.3 light-years away, while a cluster of stars observed by astronomers in 2007 is more than 1 billion light-years away.

light-year

A measure of the distance that light travels in a year; one light-year is the equivalent of nearly 6 trillion miles.

Because of their ability to observe stars and planets that are much too distant for probes to reach, telescopes play a vital role in space research. They help scientists answer questions such as how the universe formed, what it initially contained and looked like, how much it has changed over time, and when and how solar systems and galaxies formed. By unraveling mysteries of the past, scientists hope to gain additional knowledge that will help them better understand the universe and possibly determine what its future holds.

Telescopes may be on the ground at observatories or orbiting in space. Those that are ground-based are built on mountaintops where there is no obstruction of horizon views from any direction. There are other reasons why these locations are chosen, as Mike Maberry, who is with the University of Hawaii's Institute for Astronomy, explains: "The very best telescopes need the very best sites. In other words, high above the dust and pollen, things that interfere with the telescope."[48] Although many countries are home to enormous telescopes, some of the largest and most powerful in the world are located at observatories in Spain's Canary Islands, Hawaii, South Africa, Chile, and Australia, as well as the continental U.S. states of Arizona, California, and Texas.

Astronomers who work at these observatories are responsible for analyzing and interpreting the data provided by telescopes, but they rarely (if ever) study the sky by looking through them. As the Instant Hawaii Web site explains: "Unlike telescopes of the past, people do not actually observe by looking directly through modern telescopes. Instead, all observation is done by specialized electronic instruments controlled by computers."[49] In fact, at the massive Subaru Telescope, which is located on top of Hawaii's Mauna Kea, the instruments are so sensitive that during observation no one is allowed in the telescope building itself, as their body heat is enough to throw off the telescope's calibration. Instead, electronic instruments mounted on the telescope transfer information back to control room computers, where it is gathered and analyzed.

Peering into the Past

Astronomers who work with powerful telescopes have the unique ability to glimpse back in time. That is because when they gaze at stars, they are not seeing the light as it looks now, they are seeing it when it was originally created. To illustrate this concept, it helps to consider that the sun, Earth's closest star, is 91 million miles (146 million km) away. It takes just over 8 minutes for sunlight to reach Earth, so if people are viewing a sunrise or sunset, they are seeing light that was created 8 minutes before. In comparison, starlight from the farthest point in the Milky Way galaxy

Powerful Earth-based telescopes allow scientists to see trillions of miles into space. Hawaii's Suburu Telescope and Keck Observatory (I and II) are pictured at lower left along with a NASA infrared facility as Comet Hale-Bopp shoots through the night sky in 1997.

takes 100,000 years to reach Earth. With today's super-powered telescopes, astronomers are able to see stars that are much older and farther away—so distant that they formed billions of years ago, when light first began to appear in the universe. CNN journalist A. Pawlowski calls this "the closest thing we have to time machines."[50]

The 2 telescopes at the Keck Observatory, known as the Keck Twins, have proved their ability to peer back in time on many occasions. The telescopes sit atop Hawaii's Mauna Kea, a dormant volcano that towers 13,796 feet (4,205m) above sea level. Together they weigh more than 600 tons (544 metric tons), and each has 32.8 feet (10m) of mirrors. It is not possible for such an enormous piece of glass to be manufactured in one piece, so it is made up of 36 hexagonal segments that are meticulously fitted together, much like a mosaic. Astronomer Michael Richer explains why such large telescopes are so powerful: "Basically, a telescope mirror functions like a bucket in the rain: The larger the bucket, the faster you collect water. Larger telescopes allow you to collect light faster. This permits the observation of fainter sources . . . or more detailed observations that require more precise manipulation of light."[51]

One profound observation made by Keck astronomers was the existence of an enormous concentration of gas known as a Lyman-Alpha blob, which is believed to be one of the earliest remnants of a newly forming galaxy. Discovered in April 2009, scientists gave the object a name—Himiko—and they estimate that it is nearly 13 billion light-years from Earth. Taft Armandroff, who is director of the Keck Observatory, says that using the telescopes to measure the distance to Himiko was fundamental in making the discovery: "The observations show that this gigantic gaseous object formed when the Universe was only about 800 million years old, a time when astronomers have not expected to see objects like these."[52] Armandroff and his colleagues say that the gas blob is one of the most distant objects that has ever been discovered, and they are not sure of its physical origins. Two possibilities are that it could be a remnant of intensive star formation or the result of a collision between 2 young galaxies.

Scientists have discovered Lyman-Alpha blobs in the past, but the objects were found in locations where the universe was 2 to 3 billion years old. One of the most puzzling aspects of Himiko is that, as Armandroff mentioned, it is much, much older than blobs that were previously observed. In fact, its existence seems to contradict the big bang theory,

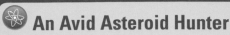

An Avid Asteroid Hunter

Robert Holmes is someone who turned a hobby into a paying job. Formerly a freelance photographer, he now works for NASA's Near Earth Object Observations program. His assignment: scour the skies for killer asteroids. Holmes fell in love with astronomy when he was 11 years old and his parents bought him his first telescope. Over the years his passion grew as he spent night after night gazing up at the skies, learning more about the cosmos as time went by. When he decided that he wanted to become an asteroid hunter, he told NASA that he would work for no pay in order to show what he could do. A year later he was offered a full-time job.

Today Holmes works from an observatory in the backyard of his home in Charleston, Illinois, on an enormous telescope that he built himself. NASA usually spots the asteroids first, then sends him the information so he can track them. He explains: "They want to keep their telescopes discovering new asteroids, so they don't have time to chase the ones they've found down again and then figure out what their orbit is." Holmes' computer-controlled telescope does the actual tracking, and he does the mathematical calculations to determine the asteroids' orbits. Once he has the data pulled together, he e-mails it to the Minor Planet Center at Harvard University, which keeps a database of potentially threatening asteroids. In 2008 Holmes tracked 6,251 asteroids, of which more than 1,000 were classified as potentially hazardous.

Quoted in Tony Reid, "Watching for Asteroids: Local Man Keeps Eyes on the Sky," *Charleston (IL) Journal Gazette and Times-Courier*, May 17, 2009. www.jg-tc.com.

which holds that the universe originated between 10 billion and 20 billion years ago from a massive explosion of matter at extremely high density and temperature. According to the theory, small objects formed first and then merged together to produce larger systems. Yet Himiko is enormous—roughly the same radius as the whole Milky Way galaxy, which is 150,000 light-years across. It is highly unusual for an object that large to have formed at such an early stage of the universe's history, so scientists are very interested in studying it further. Observations by the telescopes such as the Kecks may force them to reevaluate prevailing theories about how the universe and galaxies formed.

Outsmarting the Atmosphere

The Keck Twins and other large telescopes are equipped with a kind of sophisticated technology known as adaptive optics (AO), which is designed to overcome atmospheric distortion. In the past the effectiveness of ground-based telescopes was hampered by Earth's atmosphere, which is more than 18 miles (30km) thick and interferes with clear visibility in the sky. Scientists say that the visual effect of looking at the sky through the atmosphere can be compared with looking at an object through a glass of water. An example of atmospheric distortion is that stars seem to be twinkling in the night sky, when in fact peering at them through the atmosphere just makes them look as though they are. This causes problems for scientists, as the European Southern Observatory explains: "This turbulence causes the stars to twinkle in a way that delights poets but frustrates astronomers, since it blurs the finest details of the cosmos."[53]

> **adaptive optics**
>
> A kind of technology that enables ground-based telescopes to compensate for distortion from Earth's atmosphere.

The AO system uses computer-controlled flexible mirrors to compensate for the distortion to light as it passes through the atmosphere. Another feature of the most advanced systems is their ability to shoot laser beams into a thin layer of sodium atoms in the lower atmosphere to form a "guide star." By monitoring this artificial star, the system can determine how the air is churning around it and make necessary adjustments—more than a thousand times per second—to compensate for the atmospheric distortion. "It's incredible to see in practice," says astronomer Scott Fisher. "When the AO system is off, you see a nice, pretty star that looks a little fuzzy. Turn the AO on, and the star just goes *phonk!* and collapses to a tiny point."[54]

The Magnificent Hubble

Space-based telescopes such as the Hubble need no instruments to compensate for Earth's atmosphere because they are in orbit high above it. Undoubtedly the most famous of all orbiting telescopes, the Hubble has been scouring the universe since 1990. In the years since it was launched, it has made about 800,000 observations and taken at least 500,000 images of more than 25,000 celestial objects. One example of a Hubble discovery involved an astronomical phenomenon known as R-136. R-136 is a cluster of stars packed so densely together that scientists had long believed it was a single star. Thanks to Hubble photography, they realized that their theory was incorrect. Photographs showed that R-136 was actually a grouping of more than 60 stars, most likely some of the youngest that had ever been observed in the universe.

Defining R-136 as a star cluster was just one of Hubble's innumerable observations since it has been in orbit. The *Smithsonian Atlas of Space Exploration* offers an encapsulated version of what the Hubble has accomplished over the years:

> The telescope has documented in color detail the births and deaths of bright celestial objects. It provided visual proof that pancake-shaped dust disks around young stars are common, suggesting that the raw materials for planet formation are in place. The orbiting telescope showed for the first time that jets of material rising from embryonic stars emanate from the centers of disks of dust and gas, thus turning what was previously merely theory into an observed reality.[55]

In October 2009 NASA scientists announced that data from the Hubble Space Telescope had detected a giant planet that was bigger than Jupiter and was orbiting a sunlike star about 150 light-years away from Earth. Dubbed HD 209458B, the planet was determined to be uninhabitable but had the same basic chemistry that could potentially support life if it were a terrestrial planet rather than a hot, gaseous one. NASA researcher Mark Swain explains the significance of this finding:

> It's the second planet outside our solar system in which water, methane and carbon dioxide have been found, which are potentially important for biological processes in habitable planets. Detecting organic compounds in two exoplanets [planets beyond Earth's solar system] now raises the possibility that it will become commonplace to find planets with molecules that may be tied to life.[56]

Kepler and Spitzer

The Kepler space telescope is also searching for exoplanets. In fact, its nickname is "planet hunter" because tracking down these faraway objects is its primary mission. Launched in March 2009 and operational the following May, Kepler will spend at least four years searching for terrestrial planets that are Earth-sized and smaller. During its hunting expedition, Kepler will continuously scan more than 100,000 stars, as NASA project manager James Fanson explains: "If Kepler got into a staring contest, it would win. The spacecraft is ready to stare intently at the same stars for several years so that it can precisely measure the slightest changes in their brightness caused by planets."[57] Fanson is referring to a phenomenon known as transiting, which occurs when a planet crosses in front of a star and partially blocks its light. If Kepler detects any dimming in starlight, it is a sign that a planet has been discovered crossing its star's path.

exoplanet

A planet outside of Earth's solar system that orbits a sunlike star.

transiting

The passage of a planet across the path of a star, which causes a pronounced dimming in starlight.

The ultimate goal for Kepler is to find planets similar to Earth, since they are the most likely to harbor some sort of life. Because life cannot exist without water, Kepler's search will focus on planets that orbit stars at a far enough distance that temperatures would be conducive to the existence of lakes and oceans. Astronomer Geoffrey Marcy, who himself is a planet hunter, shares his enthusiasm for the mission: "The reason I get up in the morning is to find Earths. . . . We're on the verge of answering a question that was posed by the ancient Greeks more than 2,000 years ago. I'm not joking when I say it makes the hairs stand up on the back of my neck."[58] NASA hopes that by the time Kepler's mission is complete, it will have spotted about 50 Earthlike planets.

Another space telescope that is hunting for planets is the Spitzer. It obtains its images by detecting infrared (heat) energy that is radiated by objects in space. According to NASA, most infrared energy is blocked by the Earth's atmosphere, so it cannot be observed from the ground. Spitzer is the largest infrared telescope in the world, and it has accomplished a great deal since its launch in 2003. A whimsical article on NASA's Web site has a "quote" from Spitzer about its many discoveries:

> I hate to brag, but I was the first telescope to see actual light from an exoplanet. I was also the first to split that light up into a spectrum. Oh, sorry, there I go again with the techie talk. Light is made up of lots of different wavelengths in the same way that a rainbow is made up of different colors. I was able to split an exoplanet's light up into its various infrared wavelengths. This spectral information teaches us about planets' atmospheres.[59]

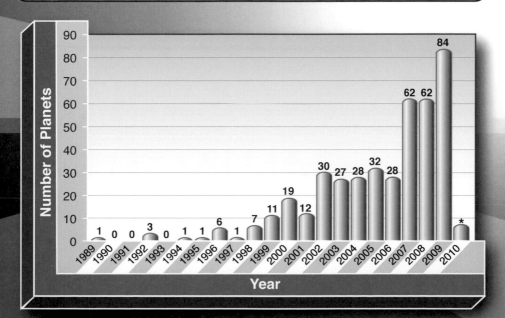

The Search for Earthlike Planets

The planet-hunting Kepler space telescope has found more than 400 exoplanets, planets outside Earth's solar system, but none so far have the right components for life. However, astronomers believe they are on the verge of finding Earthlike planets where life could develop or may have developed sometime in the past. The explosion of exoplanet discoveries in recent years increases the likelihood of finding an Earth-sized planet in a habitable zone.

*Seven exoplanets were found as of January 6, 2010.

Source: *U.S. News & World Report,* Seth Borenstein, "Astonomers: We Could Find Earth-Like Planets Soon," January 7, 2010.

In October 2009 Spitzer made a discovery that astounded scientists: an enormous ring around Saturn that they had never seen before. The ring, which is larger than any of the planet's other rings, would have been difficult to see with visible-light telescopes (those that collect and magnify light) because the dust and ice particles that make it up are spread over such a vast area. Spitzer was able to sense the glow of the cool dust because cool objects shine when exposed to infrared radiation. University of Virginia astronomer Anne Verbiscer calls the new finding "one supersized ring" and credits Spitzer's infrared technology for spotting it: "The particles are so far apart that if you were to stand in the ring, you wouldn't even know it." Verbiscer explains why Spitzer succeeded where other telescopes could not: "By focusing on the glow of the rings' cool dust, Spitzer made it easy to find."[60]

X-Ray Vision

Infrared technology played a major role in another scientific discovery that was announced in October 2009: the most distant galaxy cluster that has ever been observed. Galaxy clusters are groups of galaxies that are bound together by gravity, and they are the largest gravitationally bound objects in the universe. Known as JKCS041, the cluster is located more than 10 billion light-years away, which means that it formed when the universe was only about one-quarter of its present age. Galaxy clusters are often first detected with infrared technology that can reveal their component gases, and this was the case with JKCS041. The United Kingdom Infrared Telescope originally detected it in 2006, and the cluster's distance was subsequently confirmed by other infrared observations. Some pieces of the puzzle were still missing, however. The possibility existed that it was not a galaxy cluster at all but rather a blend of different groups of galaxies.

> **galaxy clusters**
>
> Groups of galaxies that are bound together by gravity.

This theory was refuted when a satellite known as the Chandra X-ray Observatory provided the final pieces of evidence. The world's most powerful X-ray telescope, Chandra detected hot gas between the galaxies, which was the first sign that it was an actual cluster. Measurements of characteristics such as composition, mass, and temperature confirmed that theory. Scientists are excited about this finding be-

The Man Behind the Telescope

When Edwin Hubble first went to work at the Mount Wilson Observatory in 1919, he used what was then the largest, most sophisticated telescope in the world: the Hooker. At the time, most astronomers believed that the universe and the Milky Way galaxy were one and the same. In other words, the Milky Way was the universe. But as Hubble continued to study the skies, he wondered whether the universe was much, much larger than scientists thought. In 1923 and 1924 he used the Hooker telescope to examine distant, faint clouds of light in the universe known as nebulae. He could see individual stars within them, and concluded that the nebulae were galaxies that were totally separate from the Milky Way.

Over the following years Hubble calculated the distances to many galaxies, some of which were hundreds of millions of light-years from Earth. He found that the farther away galaxies were, the faster they appeared to move away—proof that the universe was expanding at an accelerated rate. This discovery formed the basis of the big bang theory, which states that the universe began with a massive explosion of matter at extremely high density and temperature and has continued to expand ever since. For all that he contributed to the field of astronomy up until his death in 1953, he was honored by having the Hubble Space Telescope named after him.

cause it has furthered their understanding of the universe's evolution by providing more information about its early history. Astronomer Ben Maughan explains: "This discovery is exciting because it is like finding a Tyrannosaurus Rex fossil that is much older than any other known. One fossil might just fit in with our understanding of dinosaurs, but if you found many more, you would have to start rethinking how dinosaurs evolved. The same is true for galaxy clusters and our understanding of cosmology."[61]

Continuing the Quest

Space research depends on data from numerous sources, and powerful telescopes play a vital role. Enormous ground-based telescopes study stars and planets in order to expand scientists' understanding of the universe and have made many remarkable discoveries over the years. Telescopes orbiting in space scour the skies in a relentless search for answers to the mysteries of the cosmos and to look for Earthlike planets that could potentially sustain life. As this worldwide star-gazing continues, additional discoveries will be made and scientific knowledge will expand even more. As a result, the universe will likely be a little less mysterious tomorrow than it is today.

Space Research in the Future

In a September 5, 2009, speech in San Diego, California, NASA administrator Charles Bolden spoke about his vision for the future of space research. He stated: "Some believe that Apollo was the end of exploration. . . . I believe, however, that the age of grand exploration didn't end with Apollo at all. America has exploration in its DNA, and NASA will continue that proud tradition long into the future. I believe, in fact, that the future of exploration is bright, and that great journeys are still to come."[62] Scientists often disagree about what that next "great journey" should be. Many are convinced that the first priority should be a return voyage to the moon, where astronauts could build a settlement to establish a sustainable, long-term human presence. Doing so could facilitate lunar exploration, and could also serve as a permanent launch outpost for missions that travel into deep space.

Going back to the moon became one of NASA's biggest priorities after former president George W. Bush announced his vision for space research in 2004. This became the catalyst for the development of the Constellation program, which NASA said would open up a new generation of space research. Constellation was made up of four parts: the *Orion* spacecraft, which would be large enough to accommodate a crew of six astronauts; the *Ares 1* rocket and the much larger and more powerful *Ares 5* rocket; and a vehicle that would carry astronauts to and from the lunar surface. The plan for the first test flight was to travel to the International Space Station, which NASA anticipated would occur sometime in 2014. If that was successful, an actual moon mission would follow, possibly by the year 2020.

A Radical Shift in Direction

NASA's priorities for space research changed drastically in April 2010 with President Obama's speech about his vision for America's space program. He announced that the moon mission would be scrapped, along with the bulk of the Constellation program. A key factor in

Obama's decision was massive cost overruns and substantial delays that continued to push back target dates so the first moon mission would likely not happen until at least 2028. Charles Bolden shares his thoughts about why the change in priorities was necessary: "As much as we would like it not to be the case . . . the truth is that we were not on a path to get back to the moon's surface. And as we focused so much of our effort and funding on just getting to the Moon, we were neglecting investments in the key technologies that would be required to go beyond."[63]

Although the Constellation program was canceled the *Orion* was retained, but it will no longer be a lunar spacecraft. Instead, it will be redesigned for use as an emergency craft for astronauts who are living

Astronaut Buzz Aldrin, pictured here walking on the moon's surface in 1969, supports President Obama's proposal for the future of NASA and U.S. space exploration. The priority, he says, should be research that will enable humans to travel far beyond the moon.

at the International Space Station. The development of the scaled-back *Orion* was elevated to a high priority because of the retirement of the space shuttle fleet at the end of 2010. Until a new spacecraft is built, astronauts will need to travel to and from the ISS on Russian spacecraft.

Obama's cancellation of moon missions was met with vastly different reactions, with some scientists denouncing it and others expressing their support. One who was strongly in favor of the change was Buzz Aldrin, a retired astronaut who was the second person to walk on the moon as a member of the historic *Apollo* 11 mission in 1969. Aldrin is still as passionate as ever about space research but is against returning to the moon. He shared his thoughts in a letter to President Obama after the space program announcement was made:

> As an Apollo astronaut, I know the importance of always pushing new frontiers as we explore space. The truth is, that we have already been to the Moon—some 40 years ago. A near-term focus on lowering the cost of access to space and on developing key, cutting-edge technologies to take us further, faster, is just what our Nation needs to maintain its position as the leader in space exploration for the rest of this century. We need to be in this for the long haul . . . to again be pushing the boundaries to achieve new and challenging things beyond Earth.[64]

The Lure of the Red Planet

Recommendations by the U.S. Human Space Flight Plans Committee, which had been commissioned by the White House to do an in-depth study of the space program, factored heavily into Obama's decision. In an October 2009 report, the committee stated that the program was on an "unsustainable trajectory" because it had been "perpetuating the perilous practice of pursuing goals that do not match allocated resources."[65]

In spite of these cautionary words, committee members made it clear that they supported NASA's goals for space research. They also expressed that missions to Mars should be a priority for the future, as the authors wrote: "Mars is unquestionably the most scientifically interesting destination in the inner solar system, with a history much like Earth's. It possesses resources, which can be used for life support and propellants. If humans are ever to live for long periods on another planetary surface, it is likely to be on Mars."[66] In his speech, Obama said that he believed astronauts could be sent to orbit Mars by the mid-2030s, and that a landing on the planet would be the next step.

> ### propellant
> A substance that is capable of propelling or moving an object, usually involving a chemical reaction.

Although a mission carrying humans to Mars is a long-term goal, it is one that many scientists are passionate about and have been for years. As robotic probes have continued to make new discoveries, such as confirming that the planet once had abundant water, the excitement about Mars has continued to escalate. One of the great mysteries of the red planet has always been whether some form of life exists there or existed in the past—and in 2009 NASA scientists announced a discovery that may have confirmed this.

Through observations of Mars with infrared telescopes and the high-powered Keck twin telescopes, a team of scientists found signs of plentiful methane gas in the Martian atmosphere. Much of the methane in Earth's atmosphere is produced by microbes that exist within soils and inside the digestive systems of mammals, so the presence of the gas on Mars could signal the existence of some form of life. NASA states that if microscopic Martian life is producing the methane, it likely resides far beneath the planet's surface where it is warm enough for liquid water to exist. But detection of methane is not necessarily an indicator of life because the gas is also produced through natural geological processes. Still, this is an intriguing finding and one that scientists plan to study further. Perhaps when human explorers someday land on Mars, they will be able to solve such mysteries.

Future Asteroid Missions

Because a voyage carrying humans to Mars is such a monumental undertaking, many scientists, as well as President Obama, are convinced that the first mission should be to an asteroid. Preliminary studies by NASA have shown that this is feasible. According to Rob Landis, who headed up the research, telescopes have identified at least 9 asteroids that could be reached by a spacecraft that is designed to carry astronauts long distances. The round-trip journey would take an estimated 90 to 180 days, which is much longer than the 6 days it takes to get to and from the moon, but Landis says the extra time would be well worth it.

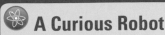

A Curious Robot

Mars has long fascinated scientists, primarily because it is more similar to Earth than any other planet. Probes have studied it from space, robots have roamed its surface, and in the process scientific knowledge has grown exponentially. In 2011 another spacecraft will head toward the red planet carrying the most sophisticated rover yet. The rover's official name is the Mars Science Laboratory, but NASA refers to it as *Curiosity*. Unlike previous rover missions, *Curiosity* will not travel on top of a lander, hit the surface encased in airbags, and bounce until it stops. Instead, a descent vehicle called Sky Crane will gently lower the rover via cables, which will then be cut once the rover's wheels touch the Martian surface.

The small, car-size rover will have a much greater range than *Spirit* and *Opportunity,* as well as more instruments, such as those that can observe Martian weather and measure cosmic radiation that bombards the planet's surface. Its high-resolution camera can photograph and videotape geological structures and features such as craters, gullies, and dunes. It will also be outfitted with a laser beam that allows it to zap rocks and then analyze the vaporized material on the spot. *Curiosity*'s mission is to search for organic molecules that are the chemical building blocks of life. NASA's Joy Crisp explains: "We want to find out whether Mars' environment was, or still is, capable of harboring life."

Quoted in Dauna Coulter, "A Mars Rover Named 'Curiosity,'" Science@NASA, October 30, 2009. http://science.nasa.gov.

A September 2009 article on the Space.com Web site explains the value of an asteroid mission:

Missions to asteroids would be useful to characterize and sample them. This would be important as early preparation to use some yet undetermined system if the need ever arose to divert an asteroid to save Earth from a devastating impact. Some asteroids are solid bodies, while others are rubble piles of loose rock, making samples and close up characterization useful for diversion studies that would differ depending upon the type of asteroid threatening Earth.[67]

One advantage to landing on asteroids is that, unlike the moon, they have very low gravity. Thus a spacecraft could conceivably fly to an asteroid, pull up right next to it, and continue to hover there. Astronauts could then climb out of the spacecraft, step onto the asteroid, and begin exploring. No lander would be necessary, which would save millions of dollars.

Scientists say that there are a number of reasons why it would be useful for astronauts to explore asteroids, one of which is their monetary value. Metallic asteroids are composed of the same materials as Earth, meaning that they are filled with minerals and other natural resources that could potentially be mined. According to Paul A. Heckert, who is a physics and astronomy professor at Western Carolina University, many asteroids contain metals such as iron, nickel, platinum, and gold. One asteroid known as 1986 DA contains precious metals that, if mined, could be worth more than $25 trillion, Heckert says. He writes: "The market value for a single moderate sized asteroid is considerably more than the entire accumulated US national debt."[68]

The Manned Versus Unmanned Debate

Many scientists share the vision of humans exploring asteroids and eventually traveling to planets such as Mars. This is controversial, however, because some argue that probes can accomplish as much as humans for less cost and at lower risk. This is the perspective of Steven Weinberg, a Nobel Prize laureate who is a physics and astronomy professor at the University of Texas. He writes:

> Manned missions to space are incredibly expensive and don't serve any important purpose. It isn't a good way of doing science, and funds are being drained from the real science that NASA does. Sending people to space may be a great show, [but] so much of what you do has to be built around the necessity of keeping people safe and alive that science takes a second place. Above all, it's an incredible waste of money.[69]

Robert Park, who is a physicist at the University of Maryland, shares Weinberg's opinion. Although Park is passionate about space research and agrees that Mars should be a high priority, he does not believe that humans should make those journeys. In his opinion, probes are perfectly capable of accomplishing the missions on their own. In fact, he argues that robotic missions are *more* effective than manned missions. He writes:

> We already have robotic explorers on Mars. They are doing fine. They never complain about the cold nights. They live on sunshine. You can't do that with humans. We have much better explorers there than we could conceivably imagine putting on Mars if we use humans. What are we after? What are we looking for in space? There is nothing that we can bring back from Mars that would begin to justify the cause of going there. The only thing we can bring back is knowledge, and we can bring knowledge back better with robots.[70]

Some believe the future of space research lies with human explorers while others say that robotic explorers such as the Mars rover (pictured here in a computer illustration) represent the best hope for acquiring new knowledge about space. In all likelihood, both will play a role in ongoing space research.

Yet many other scientists are convinced that humans *should* travel into space. While few would argue about the invaluable role probes play in space research, they are convinced that there should be a balance between manned and unmanned missions, rather than one being viewed as more valuable than the other. According to Joseph Shoer, who is a science and technology researcher, human space exploration opens up new challenges that will need to be overcome. He says that by tackling those challenges, unexpected solutions could be discovered that solve different, perhaps unrelated, problems. He writes: "We may find that our efforts have uncovered things with direct applications back home, or that we learn of a wholly unknown branch of science." Shoer adds that scientific accomplishments can be achieved by both humans and robots. "But robots come nowhere near matching the perceptive ability, flexibility, problem-solving skills, broad knowledge base, ability to shift focus, and physical maneuverability of a human being. I would also argue that a human scientist's sense of wonder would be an asset on Mars or beyond."[71]

Futuristic Threat Assessment

While missions that send humans and robotic probes into space are among the highest priorities, space research is also moving in other directions. For example, new technology is being developed that is designed to keep a close watch on asteroids and comets because both pose potential dangers to Earth. One example is Pan-STARRS, which is being constructed on top of an inactive volcano known as Haleakala on the Hawaiian island of Maui. As of December 2009, 1 telescope was operational, and by the time the observatory is complete, there will be a total of 4. The system will have 3 to 16 times the collective power of current near-Earth object telescopes and will be capable of zeroing in on asteroids that are significantly fainter than today's telescopes are able to see.

near-earth object

Asteroids, comets, or large meteoroids that travel relatively close to Earth.

Each Pan-STARRS telescope will train its eye on a patch of sky for about 30 seconds, and then move to another. By photographing 1,000 segments every night, the telescope will be able to image the entire sky once a week. By using 4 telescopes instead of 1, astronomers hope to

Intercepting an Asteroid

Because of the threat posed by asteroids, scientists have studied ways to prevent the flying rocks from striking Earth. In August 2009 a team of British scientists announced that they had designed a deflection device that could potentially protect the planet from an asteroid strike. Known as a gravity tractor, the idea was originally conceived by NASA scientists Edward Lu and Stanley Love. The device would weigh an estimated 20 tons (18 metric tons) and would work by utilizing the natural force of gravity.

If scientists determined that an asteroid was on a definite collision course with Earth, the gravity tractor would be launched into space 15 to 20 years ahead of the predicted strike date. It would make the long journey to the asteroid's location, intercept it, and position itself close to the object's surface. Then it would thrust its engines in the direction it wanted the asteroid to go. If the maneuver worked as planned, the gravitational force created by the close proximity of the spacecraft would pull the asteroid out of its orbit, thereby changing its trajectory so it headed away from Earth and no longer posed a threat.

get a more accurate picture of space, which will allow them to identify potential threats years in advance. NASA astronomer David Morrison states that "the rate of discoveries is going to ramp up. We're going to see discoveries being made at 50 to 100 times the current rate."[72] To date, astronomers have tracked an estimated 100,000 asteroids, while Pan-STARRS will be capable of spotting and cataloging more than 10 million.

Superpowered Telescopes

Other telescopes are also being developed that scientists say will be far more powerful than those in operation today. For example, the European Extremely Large Telescope (E-ELT) will be 4 times larger than any telescope that has ever been built. Construction is expected to start in 2010, and the goal is for it to be operational by 2018. Although the telescope's location has not yet been determined, it will likely be located in Chile or the Canary Islands. When it is complete, the E-ELT's mirror will be massive—as large as 5 buses lined up from end to end. Composed of more than 900 hexagonal segments, the E-ELT will have more glass than all other telescopes in the world put together. An April 2009 article in London's *Daily Telegraph* explains what such an enormous expanse of glass will mean: "It is expected to be so powerful that if astronomers were to use it to peer at the Moon, they would be able to see the car sized lunar rover that was left on the moon by astronauts during the Apollo missions."[73]

habitable zone

A region in space where conditions exist that could be favorable for the existence of life.

Astronomers say that the massive telescope will be able to spot rocky Earth-like planets that are up to 100 million miles (161 million km) away, in an area known as the habitable zone. Within this zone planets are far enough away from the stars they orbit that they are not too hot to support life, but also not so far away from their stars that the climate would be too cold. Once the E-ELT is fully operational, it will be the first time that planets beyond Earth's solar system will have been seen using light from their surface. As the *Telegraph* article states, "Current telescopes are not powerful enough to detect even giant planets in this way as the light they reflect is overwhelmed by far brighter stars."[74] By analyzing the light that is reflected from these planets, astronomers may very well be able to determine which gases are in their atmosphere, whether water or vegetation exists on the surface, and perhaps even whether there is life on the planet. Because the E-ELT will be so powerful and equipped with highly sophisticated adaptive optics technology, the scientists who are developing it believe that it may make space telescopes obsolete in the future.

What Tomorrow Holds

Whether it involves scouring the skies for planets, stars, and asteroids or sending humans to the moon or Mars, the future of space research will undoubtedly present challenges as well as yield more exciting discoveries. According to Roger D. Launius and Andrew K. Johnston, authors of the *Smithsonian Atlas of Space Exploration*, space research has changed the way that humanity views itself. They write: "It brought us knowledge and understanding to be sure, but it also stretched our imaginations and made us believe that anything we set our minds to we could accomplish." They add that the thrill of space and all the mysteries that it holds will continue to drive space research in the years to come: "A limitless future for humanity in space remains the critical but elusive goal of the space age. Russian spaceflight pioneer Konstantin Tsiolkovsky said it best: 'The Earth is the cradle of the mind, but we cannot remain forever in the cradle.' Space exploration has taught us that this cradle is not a cage and that we can leave it."[75]

Source Notes

Introduction: "Discovery, Science, Innovation"

1. Quoted in Joel Achenbach, "Satellite Shows Signs of Water at Moon's Pole," *Washington Post*, November 14, 2009. www.washingtonpost.com.

2. Quoted in Stephen J. Dubner, "Is Space Exploration Worth the Cost? A Freakonomics Quorum," *New York Times*, January 11, 2008. http://freakonomics.blogs.nytimes.com.

3. Quoted in Science Daily, "Icy Moons of Saturn and Jupiter May Have Conditions Needed for Life," December 16, 2009. www.sciencedaily.com.

4. Charles Bolden, "Remarks by NASA Administrator Charles Bolden," September 5, 2009. www.nasa.gov.

Chapter One: What Is Space Research?

5. Stephen Hawking, "The Final Frontier," *Cosmos*, September 24, 2008. www.cosmosmagazine.com.

6. Quoted in Kate Ravilious, "Giant 'Space Tornadoes' Spark Auroras on Earth," *National Geographic*, April 24, 2009. http://news.nationalgeographic.com.

7. National Aeronautics and Space Administration, "Colliding Auroras Produce an Explosion of Light," December 17, 2009. www.nasa.gov.

8. National Aeronautics and Space Administration, "Mars, Water & Life." http://marsprogram.jpl.nasa.gov.

9. Quoted in James Owen, "First Habitable Earthlike Planet Found, Experts Say," *National Geographic*, April 24, 2007. http://news.nationalgeographic.com.

10. Owen, "First Habitable Earthlike Planet Found, Experts Say."

11. Quoted in Dubner "Is Space Exploration Worth the Cost? A Freakonomics Quorum."

12. Quoted in Jennifer Collings, "CALIPSO Finds Smoke at High Altitudes Down Under," NASA Earth Observatory, March 5, 2009. http://earthobservatory.nasa.gov.

13. Collings, "CALIPSO Finds Smoke at High Altitudes Down Under."

14. Quoted in Charles Q. Choi, "Opening Up Asteroids to Space Settlement?" *Ad Astra*, Winter 2007. www.nss.org.

15. Quoted in Tony Reid, "Watching for Asteroids: Local Man Keeps Eyes on the Sky," *Charleston (IL) Journal Gazette/Times-Courier*, May 17, 2009. www.jg-tc.com.

16. Joan Vernikos, "Human Exploration of Space: Why, Where, What For?" *Hippokratia*, August 2008. www.ncbi.nlm.nih.gov.

17. Vernikos, "Human Exploration of Space."

18. James Geiger, "Telemedicine Usage Exploding—eICU, daVinci Robotic Surgery," Sweet Smell of Success's Blog, August 6, 2009. http://thesweetsmellofsuccess.wordpress.com.

19. Geiger, "Telemedicine Usage Exploding—eICU, daVinci Robotic Surgery."

20. Vernikos, "Human Exploration of Space."

21. Quoted in Kevin Joy, "Ex-Astronaut Glenn Backs Space Research," *Columbus (OH) Dispatch*, January 22, 2008. www.dispatch.com.

Chapter Two: Probing the Universe

22. National Aeronautics and Space Administration, "MESSENGER: Mission Overview," November 2007. http://messenger.jhuapl.edu.

23. Quoted in National Aeronautics and Space Administration, "Messenger's Final Flyby of Mercury," September 23, 2009. http://science.nasa.gov.

24. Planetary Society, "Space Topics: Cassini-Huygens," 2009. www.planetary.org.

25. Quoted in Science Daily, "Celebrating the Fifth Anniversary of Huygens' Titan Touchdown," January 15, 2010. www.sciencedaily.com.

26. National Aeronautics and Space Administration, "Discovery Mission: Deep Impact," September 16, 2009. http://discovery.nasa.gov.

27. National Aeronautics and Space Administration, "Dawn: A Journey to the Beginning of the Solar System," 2010. http://dawn.jpl.nasa.gov.

28. Tony Phillips, "Monster Waves on the Sun Are Real," Science@NASA, November 24, 2009. http://science.nasa.gov.

29. Erica Hupp, Dwayne Brown, Rani Gran, and Lynn Chandler, "NASA Satellites Will Improve Understanding of the Sun," *NASA News*, October 18, 2006. www.nasa.gov.

30. Science Daily, "Solar Storms: Coronal Mass Ejections Viewed in Detail by NASA Spacecraft," April 15, 2009. www.sciencedaily.com.

31. Quoted in Dwayne Brown and Nancy Neal Jones, "NASA Spacecraft Ready to Explore Outer Solar System," National Aeronautics and Space Administration news release, October 6, 2008. www.nasa.gov.

32. Quoted in Dwayne Brown and Nancy Neal Jones, "IBEX Explores Galactic Frontier, Releases First-Ever All-Sky Map," National Aeronautics and Space Administration news release, October 15, 2009. www.nasa.gov.

33. David McComas, "IBEX Interstellar Boundary Explorer," NASA Southwest Research Institute, October 15, 2009. http://ibex.swri.edu.

Chapter Three: Living and Working in Space

34. Quoted in William Harwood, "Japanese Science Platform Attached to Space Station," CNET News, July 18, 2009. http://news.cnet.com.

35. Quoted in Cheryl L. Mansfield, "A Station Celebration," NASA International Space Station, December 4, 2008. www.nasa.gov.

36. Steven Roy, "Sailing with the Stars: International Space Station," NASA Blog, October 22, 2009. http://blogs.nasa.gov.

37. National Aeronautics and Space Administration, *Research in Space: Facilities on the International Space Station*, August 2009. www.nasa.gov.

38. Quoted in Katherine Trinidad, Ashley Edwards, and Kelly Humphries, "Space Research May Help Explain Salmonella Illness," National Aeronautics and Space Administration news release, March 11, 2009. www.nasa.gov.

39. National Aeronautics and Space Administration, *International Space Station Science Research Accomplishments During the Assembly Years: 2000–2008*, June 2009. www.nasa.gov.

40. Lori Meggs, "Learning How Materials Work in Space to Make Them Better on Earth," Science Daily, September 22, 2009. www.sciencedaily.com.

41. Quoted in Meggs, "Learning How Materials Work in Space to Make Them Better on Earth."

42. National Aeronautics and Space Administration, "Fact Sheet: Crew Earth Observations (CEO)," August 28, 2009. www.nasa.gov.

43. National Aeronautics and Space Administration, *Research in Space*.

44. U.S. Human Spaceflight Plans Committee, *Summary Report*, October 22, 2009. www.nasa.gov.

45. Barack Obama, "Remarks by the President on Space Exploration in the 21st Century," April 15, 2010. www.nasa.gov.

46. Roy, "Sailing with the Stars: International Space Station."

Chapter Four: Eyes on the Universe

47. Michio Kaku, "Jupiter Gets a Black Eye," *Wall Street Journal*, July 23, 2009. http://online.wsj.com.

48. Quoted in Steven Tonthat, "Impact Objects," *Maui News*, September 1, 2008. www.mauinews.com.

49. Instant Hawaii, "Anatomy of a Telescope—Subaru Telescope Project on Mauna Kea," 2008. www.instanthawaii.com.

50. A. Pawlowski, "Telescopes to Show Universe Soon After Big Bang," CNN, August 18, 2009. www.cnn.com.

51. Quoted in Irene Klotz, "World's Largest Telescope Acts Like Big Bucket," Discovery Channel, July 23, 2009. http://dsc.discovery.com.

52. Quoted in W.M. Keck Observatory, "Mysterious Space Blob Discovered at Cosmic Dawn," April 23, 2009. http://keckobservatory.org.

53. European Southern Observatory, "Adaptive Optics," September 22, 2009. www.eso.org.

54. Quoted in Timothy Ferris, "Cosmic Vision," *National Geographic*, July 2009. http://ngm.nationalgeographic.com.

55. Roger D. Launius and Andrew K. Johnston, *Smithsonian Atlas of Space Exploration*. New York: HarperCollins, 2009, p. 83.

56. Quoted in National Aeronautics and Space Administration, "Mission News," October 20, 2009. www.nasa.gov.

57. Quoted in Space.com, "NASA's Planet Hunter Starts Hunting," May 13, 2009. www.space.com.

58. Quoted in Michael D. Lemonick, "Kepler Space Probe: A Shot at Finding New Earths," *Time*, August 6, 2009. www.time.com.

59. Whitney Claven, "If Spitzer Could Talk: An Interview with NASA's Coolest Space Telescope," National Aeronautics and Space Administration, May 5, 2009. www.spitzer.caltech.edu.

60. Quoted in National Aeronautics and Space Administration, "NASA Space Telescope Discovers Largest Ring Around Saturn," October 6, 2009. www.nasa.gov.

61. Quoted in Janet Anderson and Megan Watzke, "Galaxy Cluster Smashes Distance Record," National Aeronautics and Space Administration news release, October 22, 2009. www.nasa.gov.

Chapter Five: Space Research in the Future

62. Charles Bolden, "Remarks by NASA Administrator Charles Bolden," National Aeronautics and Space Administration, September 5, 2009. www.nasa.gov.

63. Charles Bolden, "Statement by Charlie Bolden, NASA Administrator," National Aeronautics and Space Administration, February 1, 2010. www.nasa.gov.

64. Buzz Aldrin, "Statement from Buzz Aldrin: A New Direction in Space," February 1, 2010. www.whitehouse.gov.

65. U.S. Human Spaceflight Plans Committee, *Summary Report*.

66. U.S. Human Spaceflight Plans Committee, *Summary Report*.

67. Craig Covault, "NASA's New Spaceships Could Tag-Team Asteroid," Space.com, September 2, 2009. www.space.com.

68. Paul A. Heckert, "Economic Impact of Asteroids & Space Exploration," Suite 101, January 8, 2010. http://space-exploration.suite101.com.

69. Steven Weinberg, participant in Kenneth R. Fletcher, "Debating Manned Moon Missions," *Smithsonian*, July 2008. www.smithsonianmag.com.

70. Robert Park, participant in Kenneth R. Fletcher, "Debating Manned Moon Missions," *Smithsonian*, July 2008. www.smithsonianmag.com.

71. Joseph Shoer, "Reasons for Human Space," Quantum Rocketry blog, July 31, 2009. http://josephshoer.com.

72. Quoted in Elizabeth Svoboda, "'Gravity Tractor,' Super Telescopes Enlisted to Battle Killer Asteroids," *National Geographic*, February 17, 2007. http://news.nationalgeographic.com.

73. Richard Gray, "World's Largest Telescope Will Search Heavens for Habitable Planets Like Earth," *Daily Telegraph* (London), April 4, 2009. www.telegraph.co.uk.

74. Gray, "World's Largest Telescope Will Search Heavens for Habitable Planets Like Earth."

75. Launius and Johnston, *Smithsonian Atlas of Space Exploration*, p. ix.

Facts About Space

The Sun and Moon
- The sun is the largest object in Earth's solar system and contains approximately 98 percent of the total solar system's mass.
- The temperature of the sun's core is estimated to be 27 million degrees Fahrenheit (15 million degrees C), and its surface temperature is 11,000 degrees Fahrenheit (6,100 degrees C).
- NASA states that the sun has been burning for nearly 5 billion years, and will last for another 5 billion years.
- Astrophysicist Andreas Keiling states that space tornadoes carry electrical currents of more than 100,000 amps, which is 10 times that of a lightning strike.
- The orbital speed of the moon is 2,287 miles per hour (3,680kph).
- The moon has about the same surface area as the continent of Africa.

Galaxies and Stars
- In Earth's Milky Way galaxy, the sun is just one of about 100 billion stars.
- Supergiants, the largest stars, have diameters several hundred times the size of Earth's sun.
- A galaxy called Andromeda is over 2.4 million light-years away from Earth.
- Astronomers estimate that the universe contains more than 100 billion galaxies, and each galaxy may have more than 100 billion stars.
- Black holes are the last evolutionary stage in the lifetimes of enormous stars that were at least 10 or 15 times as massive as Earth's sun.

Deep Space
- More than 300 planets have been detected beyond Earth's solar system, and these are known as exoplanets.
- In 2009 NASA's Kepler space telescope discovered a planet called HAT-P-7, which is about 1,000 light-years from Earth and is 26 times closer to its star than Earth is to the sun.

- An exoplanet known as PSR B1620-26b is estimated to be 13 billion years old, which is nearly three times the age of Earth.
- Carbonaceous asteroids, which are rich in carbon, account for more than 75 percent of the asteroids in the main asteroid belt.

Earth's Solar System
- Olympus Mons, a volcano on Mars, is the largest volcano found in the solar system. It is 370 miles (595km) across and 15 miles (24km) high.
- In 2006 members of the International Astronomical Union declared that Pluto was no longer classified as one of the planets in Earth's solar system, but rather was a dwarf planet.
- Surface temperatures on Venus are nearly 900°F (482°C).
- Neptune's winds can blow at 1,600 miles per hour (2,575kph) and are the fastest winds in the solar system.
- Jupiter has 63 moons, more than any other planet in the solar system.

International Space Station
- When the International Space Station (ISS) is complete, it will have more than 262,000 solar cells.
- A solar array on the ISS has a wingspan of 240 feet (73m), which is longer than that of a Boeing 777 jet.
- NASA states that supporting 3 crew members for 6 months on the ISS requires 4 tons (3.6 metric tons) of supplies.
- More than 50 computers control system operations on the ISS.

Related Organizations

Association of Universities for Research in Astronomy (AURA)

1212 New York Ave. NW, Suite 450
Washington, DC 20005
phone: (202) 483-2101
fax: (202) 483-2106
Web site: www.aura-astronomy.org

AURA is a consortium of universities and educational institutions, as well as other nonprofits, that operates astronomical observatories (known as centers) that serve scientific communities. Its Web site offers astronomy information and resources, sections titled Telescopes from the Ground Up and Online Explorations, news articles, and a Capture the Cosmos topic search.

Canadian Space Agency

John H. Chapman Space Centre
6767 Route de l'Aéroport
Saint-Hubert, QC J3Y 8Y9
Canada
phone: (450) 926-4800
fax: (450) 926-4352
Web site: www.asc-csa.gc.ca

The Canadian Space Agency is committed to leading the development and application of space knowledge for the benefit of Canadians, as well as citizens everywhere. Its Web site features information about space activities and astronauts, a searchable database of photographs and videos, a variety of publications, an "Astronautics Vocabulary" section, and numerous other resources of interest to people who want to know more about space exploration.

Coalition for Space Exploration

1150 Gemini Ave.
Houston, TX 77058

RELATED ORGANIZATIONS

phone: (281) 335-0200
Web site: www.spacecoalition.com

The Coalition for Space Exploration is a collaboration of space industry businesses and advocacy groups whose mission is to educate and inform the public on the value and benefits of space exploration and to help ensure that the United States will remain a leader in space, science, and technology. Its Web site features information about the accomplishments and benefits of space exploration, research papers, news releases, and the Space Coalition blog.

European Space Agency (ESA)

8-10 rue Mario Nikis
75738 Paris Cedex 15
France
phone: 33 1 5369 7654
fax: 33 1 5369 7560
e-mail: contactesa@esa.int
Web site: www.esa.int

The ESA seeks to provide for and promote cooperation among European nations in space research and technology. Its Web site features a "Life in Space" section, news releases, and a vast variety of publications about space exploration.

National Aeronautics and Space Administration (NASA)

Suite 5K39
Washington, DC 20546-0001
phone: (202) 358-0001
fax: (202) 358-4338
Web site: www.nasa.gov

NASA is the United States' primary agency for aeronautics, exploration, science, and space operations. A vast amount of information about space research is accessible through its Web site, including reports; past, present, and future space mission details; photographs, videos, and podcasts; and an extensive *World Book at NASA* collection of articles.

National Science Foundation

4201 Wilson Blvd.
Arlington, VA 22230 ı

phone: (703) 292-5111; toll-free: (800) 877-8339
e-mail: info@nsf.gov
Web site: www.nsf.gov

An agency of the U.S. government, the National Science Foundation supports all fields of fundamental science and engineering with the exception of medical sciences. Its Web site features news articles, statistics, and an Astronomy & Space Discoveries section that covers a wide array of space-related topics.

National Space Society

1155 Fifteenth St. NW, Suite 500
Washington, DC 20005
phone: (202) 429-1600
fax: (202) 530-0659
e-mail: nsshq@nss.org
Web site: www.nss.org

The National Space Society seeks to promote the type of change necessary to expand civilization beyond Earth and create settlements in space in order to benefit humanity. Its Web site offers an expansive About Space section that contains hundreds of articles, videos, photographs, and links to the Mission Blog and *Ad Astra* magazine.

Planetary Society

65 N. Catalina Ave.
Pasadena, CA 91106-2301
phone: (626) 793-5100
fax: (626) 793-5528
e-mail: tps@planetary.org
Web site: www.planetary.org

The Planetary Society is a nongovernmental, nonprofit space organization that is dedicated to exploring the solar system and seeking life beyond Earth. Its Web site features news articles, fact sheets, a collection of photographs, information about space missions, and a For Kids section that includes a number of fun activities.

Students for the Exploration and Development of Space (SEDS)

MIT Room W20-445
77 Massachusetts Ave.

Cambridge, MA 02139-4307
e-mail: seds@seds.org
Web site: www.seds.org

SEDS is an independent, student-based organization that promotes the exploration and development of space. Its Web site features a photo gallery, online discussion forums, the *NOVA* magazine, and a collection of links to many other space-related sites.

For Further Research

Books

Buzz Aldrin and Ken Abraham, *Magnificent Desolation: The Long Journey Home from the Moon.* New York: Harmony, 2009.

Steven J. Dick, ed., *America in Space: NASA's First Fifty Years.* New York: Abrams, 2007.

Philip Harris, *Space Enterprise: Living and Working Offworld in the 21st Century.* New York: Springer, 2008.

Roger D. Launius and Andrew K. Johnston, *Smithsonian Atlas of Space Exploration.* New York: HarperCollins, 2009.

Cynthia Phillips and Shana Priwer, *Space Exploration for Dummies.* Indianapolis: Wiley, 2009.

Periodicals

Fred Guterl and Eve Conant, "A Private Space Shuttle," *Newsweek International*, October 19, 2009.

Tom Jones, "A Bolder NASA: A Four-Time Shuttle Astronaut Advises the President on How to Lead in Space," *Popular Mechanics*, June 2009.

Susan J. Landers, "Space Studies Also Meet Health Needs on Earth," *American Medical News*, April 13, 2009.

Thomas Mallon, "Across the Universe (Space Exploration)," *Atlantic*, May 2009.

Glenn Harlan Reynolds, "Why I Hope There's No Life on Mars: Why Such a Spoilsport? Because Life on Mars Would Make Human Exploration Much Harder," *Popular Mechanics*, December 2008.

Web Sites

Earth Sky (www.earthsky.org). Numerous space-related articles can be found on this site, and its Space section features interviews with noted scientists who cover topics such as moon exploration, life on other planets, and the universe.

FOR FURTHER RESEARCH

How Stuff Works: Space Exploration Library (http://science.howstuff works.com/space-exploration-channel.htm). This site offers a collection of articles on such topics as the Hubble Space Telescope, NASA's greatest achievements, everyday products spawned by space research, and how moon and Mars exploration works.

Hubble Site (http://hubblesite.org). An excellent collection of information about the Hubble Space Telescope and its discoveries may be found on this site, including a photo gallery, news articles, a reference desk, a monthly guide to constellations and planets, and a special Explore Astronomy section designed for young people who are interested in space research.

On Being a Scientist: A Guide to Responsible Conduct in Research (www.nap.edu/openbook.php?record_id=12192&page=R1). This is a free, downloadable book from the National Academy of Sciences Committee on Science, Engineering, and Public Policy. The 2009 edition provides a clear explanation of the responsible conduct of scientific research. Chapters on treatment of data, mistakes and negligence, the scientist's role in society, and other topics offer invaluable insight for student researchers.

Space.com (www.space.com). This Web site features an expansive collection of stories on topics such as the International Space Station, current and future space missions, the moon and planets, meteor showers, and much more. It also features videos, online forums, and links to other space-related sites.

Space Today (www.spacetoday.org). This site offers a vast number of stories about the Hubble Space Telescope, space shuttles, space stations, satellites, planets, rockets, the solar system, and deep space.

Index

Picture Credits

Cover: iStockphoto.com
Maury Aaseng: 61
AP Images: 18
iStockphoto.com: 8, 9
Landov: 66
Photos.com: 71
Science Photo Library: 11, 13, 16, 21, 24, 30, 37, 43, 45, 47, 48, 55

About the Author

Peggy J. Parks holds a bachelor of science degree from Aquinas College in Grand Rapids, Michigan, where she graduated magna cum laude. She has written more than 90 nonfiction educational books for children and young adults. Parks lives in Muskegon, Michigan, a town that she says inspires her writing because of its location on the shores of Lake Michigan.